I do believe that in this generation we need Christian communities that are clearly convinced that the outworking of the gospel is meant to touch every aspect of our lives. The Better Way carries that conviction. Alex cuts to the heart by laying out the sobering consequences of choosing our own way. And then, with genuine joy, he expounds on the way that Jesus shows us in His Kingdom. My prayer is that this book makes it in as many hands as possible and people say "yes" to really following the Jesus way.

Pastor Drew Meyer
Author of *Discovering The Power Of Prayer*
Lead Pastor | LifePointe Church - Ames, IA

I have known Alex for many years, and I appreciate his friendship and heart for people. In writing "The Better Way" he has offered new college students a practical foundation for dealing with life on campus. He begins his chapters with real life examples we can all identify with. His honesty and vulnerability help us apply the wise lessons of God's word to our lives. I enthusiastically endorse this book. Apply its principles to your life.

Brad Lewis
Author of *Small Group University*
North Dakota Chi Alpha Director

The Better Way is an insightful combination of solid biblical theology, loving contemporary apologetics, and wise, practical counsel that offers college and university students a fresh vision of the gospel and the life it generates in those who embrace it. This call to discipleship is a sweet love offering to God's people in any stage of life, but I believe it will be especially effective as a tool for those engaging students in higher education who are attempting to sort through the things that are real, meaningful, and ultimate in life. Alex's combination of uncompromising faithfulness to Scripture and gentle, conversational tone make this book a significant resource that deserves to be in the hands of young people on as many campuses as possible.

Dr. Jeff Hubing
Author of Crucifixion and New Creation
Elder | Cross Culture Church – Chicago, IL
President of FIRE School of Ministry – Chicago

The Better Way is a fantastic resource! I would encourage anyone who is newer to faith in Jesus Christ, or considering making Jesus their Lord and Savior, to read this book and work through its questions at the end of each chapter. Alex does a great job of helping the reader gain a clearer understanding of the way of Christ. It is easy to read, scripturally sound, and chalked full of insight and wisdom. The Better Way is a "must have" resource for any pastor or leader who is discipling new believers!

Pastor Austin Weaver
Senior Associate Pastor | New Hope Church - Urbandale, IA

With great conciseness, potency, and relatability, Alex addresses the challenges of today's student and young adult. The Better Way clearly articulates that following Jesus does not mean we just dip our toes in the waters of Christianity. Instead, we must fully immerse ourselves in the way of Jesus. When we do, it changes everything. I believe the reader will better understand this truth after enjoying this book.

Pastor Steven Pavek
Chi Alpha University of Alaska (Anchorage) Director

Life is filled with potential pitfalls and our decisions and choices have undeniable consequences, both good and bad. While we all want what is best, the way we choose to live and the pathways we choose to walk will determine whether or not we will experience God's best for our lives. Alex Rosinger's book, "The Better Way," fully engages the reader in evaluating that reality. The inferior ways of humanity must be replaced with the Better Way of the Savior! Lives will be changed for God's ultimate good if the principles of this book are embraced and assimilated. Read it and be blessed. Share it and bless others!

Pastor Gary Pilcher
Lead Pastor | Berean Assembly of God - Altoona, IA

THE BETTER WAY

The Good News
OF JESUS FOR OUR WAY OF LIVING

W. Alex Rosinger

Copyright © 2024 by **W. Alex Rosinger**

All rights reserved. No portion of this book may be reproduced in any form without written permission from the publisher or author, except as permitted by U.S. copyright law.

Unless otherwise noted, Scripture quotations are taken from *The Holy Bible*, New Living Translation, copyright © 1996, 2004, 2015 by Tyndale House Foundation. Used by permission of Tyndale House Publishers, Inc., Carol Stream, Illinois 60188. All rights reserved.

Scriptures marked NIV are from THE HOLY BIBLE, NEW INTERNATIONAL VERSION®, NIV® Copyright © 1973, 1978, 1984, 2011 by Biblica, Inc.® Used by permission. All rights reserved worldwide.

Cover Design: Gades Creative Co.

The Better Way / W. Alex Rosinger – 1st ed.
ISBN 979-8882549632

This book is dedicated to the students in Chi Alpha at Iowa State University. It is a humble privilege to help teach you and live out the Better Way of Jesus with you.

May we never depart from it.

Table of Contents

INTRODUCTION ... 1

PART 1: THERE IS A BETTER WAY ... 7

CHAPTER 1: DEATH^2 - OUR OLD, TIRED WAY ... 9
CHAPTER 2: THE WAY GOD INTENDED ... 19
CHAPTER 3: THE WAY OF CORRUPTION ... 29
CHAPTER 4: THE WAY OF RELIGION ... 39
CHAPTER 5: THE WAY ... 45
CHAPTER 6: THE WAY OF THE CROSS ... 55

PART 2: LIVING THE BETTER WAY ... 65

CHAPTER 7: THE WAY OF FREEDOM ... 67
CHAPTER 8: THE WAY OF FULLNESS ... 77
CHAPTER 9: THE WAY OF RELATIONSHIP ... 91
CHAPTER 10: THE WAY OF INTIMACY ... 103
CHAPTER 11: THE WAY OF FAMILY ... 113
CHAPTER 12: THE WAY OF FAITHFULNESS ... 125
CHAPTER 13: THE WAY IS THE DESTINATION ... 135

CONCLUSION ... 145

NOTES ... 149

Introduction

"There is a way that appears to be right, but in the end it leads to death."
Proverbs 14:12 (NIV)

My freshman year of engineering school at Iowa State University was exhilarating. New place. New friends. New freedoms. New everything. And everyone else, so it seemed to me, was experiencing that same rush that comes with a new lease on life. We were finally adults in a world that was ours for the taking. We were going to leave our impact on it, and nothing was going to stop us! We were brimming with hope, wonder, and the "what if's" of a promising new life.

In the semesters following, we hurled ourselves into whatever we felt was best. The messages from our university, our peers, and the culture we were immersed in were "Be true to yourself" and "Do what makes you happy." With this encouragement, we went headlong into any activity or lifestyle that met that criteria. Some of us chased after success in our academics or career path. Others jumped into new friend circles. We took risks with new experiences and tried anything that promised to bring us pleasure. The only limiting principle was "Do what's best for yourself."

The Better Way

Fast forward three and a half years, and things were very different. The fresh faces I had seen on many of my peers had soured into a weariness. A sullenness, even. The new places had become familiar. The new freedoms turned into new burdens. The previous three and a half years had not been kind to many of my classmates and roommates. What happened? And how did it happen so quickly? At least for many, the future prospect of a new job with a big salary and zero homework was beckoning them onward through their final months of school.

Leap ahead another four years, and things had often gotten worse. The life that promised large paychecks and freedom from schoolwork proved to be more emptying than the one they had in school. Taxes had to be paid on those large paychecks. Jobs proved to be mundane and monotonous. The hours spent on homework transformed into hours bingeing TV or YouTube to fill this new hollowness. Some chose to turn to alcohol or other forms of intoxication to medicate their souls. Others ran from relationship to relationship looking for someone to pull them out of the empty void their lives were becoming, only to be pulled into someone else's void.

Some may argue that my words are an overgeneralization, but I have seen it anecdotally in the lives of many of my peers. The void is obvious. The transformation from hopeful freshman to battered soul is very real. It pains me to see it happen again and again. Unfortunately, this phenomenon is

Introduction

not limited to a select few people. As we will discuss later in this book, modern research confirms this sad reality. We are all more depressed, more lonely, more anxious, and more disconnected from each other than ever before. Life, for so many, has become empty. Clearly, our way of living is not working.

This emptying life is reality for millions of college/university students. As someone who works specifically with this demographic, I am acutely aware of how this age group cycles through year after year. That cycle means that those millions of college/university students hollowed out by life become millions of post-graduate adults in the marketplace next year. And most of those former students don't find any more fulfillment in adult life. In the meantime, there's an entire new class of millions of students beginning down the same road. This happens year after year.

If we extrapolate that experience out over decades, that means hundreds of millions of people will go the same way as their predecessors. Depressed. Anxious. Lonely. Empty. A people whose highlight in life is rushing towards a weekend filled with the cheap pleasures of entertainment, pornography, and doom scrolling. This will hollow out a society in its entirety. Indeed, it already has in many ways. Why does this seem to be the way that so many of our lives go? Certainly, this isn't the way our lives are meant to be lived!

The Better Way

In the midst of this emptying cycle, there are a few who stand out as remarkably different. They have faced the same circumstances and challenges of their peers. They have known the financial hardships of student debt. They have undergone the pressure to build an image on social media. They have gone through the bumpy transition out of college into the full-time working world. Despite these many similar conditions, their lives seem to be different. Rather than being empty, they are full. Peace is a prevailing force in their life. Joy is a regular experience. Meaning and hope have even captured the mundane of their everyday.

What makes these people so uncommon? Why are their responses to the pressures of life so notably different? What delineates between the fullness of life that they seem to have and the experience of most in our world? They have chosen a different WAY to live. What they value, what they believe, what they put their hope in, what they prioritize, what they say, what they spend their money on, what their dreams are. It's all different. Their way of living starkly contrasts the way offered by our world.

Hence, the reason for writing this book. We all, as individuals, have a choice between these two ways of living. The first is our own way, the common way of our world. This postmodern way of living is guided by the "Do what makes you most happy" platitude. This way doesn't end well. *"There is a way that*

Introduction

appears to be right, but in the end it leads to death" Proverbs 14:12 (NIV). This way leads to pain. This way leads to more suffering. This way leads to a dark end.

The other way is starkly different. It's not new. It's not innovative. In fact, it's quite ancient. It's the opposite of so many of the ways our world prescribes for us to live. Yet, it has stood the test of time. The way of Jesus, as I will propose in this book, is the better way. For me, the words from Jesus that have become representative of this better way now sit on the mantle of my home's fireplace. John 10:10 (NIV), *"I have come that they may have life, and have it to the full."* Jesus says to all who are willing to hear, "I have come to give you LIFE!" But it is His way, not our way.

That leaves you and me with a choice. I have seen the poor results of my own way, and I've decided that I want to follow Jesus's way to life. My hope is that you too choose His way to life.

For many, the idea of listening to the ways God tells us to live seems like a heavy burden. A giant list of "dos and don'ts" is what they think of when Jesus is considered. This viewpoint, however, is a distortion of Jesus's purpose and God's intention for humanity. God wants humanity to flourish. Jesus wants to give us His life. Therefore, God's ways are actually an invitation to a better way of living. Whatever He says is a better way to live, really is better! And even if my own personal life fails to live up to the ways that Jesus invites us all into, His ways will remain better. My failure would not be a failure of His ways but rather it would be a failure to live up to His way. We fall short. He does not.

Jesus says in Luke 7:35, *"But wisdom is shown to be right by the lives of those who follow it."* The outcome, the fruit, and the after-effects of our lives will demonstrate which way leads to life. By this measure, we can already evaluate outcomes of the way of life offered by this world, a life lived far less than what we were meant for. In contrast to the world, what kind of life outcomes are produced in the way of Jesus? If it's not just a list of rules, then what actually is the way of Jesus? Let us, together, look at His way in the following pages of this book. It really just might be the better way.

Part 1: There Is A Better Way

Chapter 1

Death[2] - Our Old, Tired Way

"For the wages of sin is death..." Romans 6:23

It is not very often that the apocalyptic book of the Revelation of John (the final book of the Bible) is quoted in a scientific journal of medicine, but in 1973 in "Proceedings of the Royal Society of Medicine", that is exactly what happened. The results of an experiment so frightened Dr. John Calhoun at the National Institute of Mental Health that he not only quoted the book once but four times. The potential meaning of his study had very serious implications for humanity. These implications were so drastic in the mind of this PhD-level researcher that he turned to one of the darkest predictions in the Bible. Dr. Calhoun quoted Revelation 6:8, which you should certainly read yourself, regarding the Fourth Horsemen of the Apocalypse whose name is Death. Yikes! What did he see in his research that forced him to reach for the most extreme of biblical imagery?

Years earlier, Dr. Calhoun created a place called Mouse Utopia.[1] With nearly limitless supplies of food and water, void of predators, and an abundance of open space, the ideal physical conditions were created for mice to live in. Inside of this "Mouse Utopia", Dr. Calhoun placed four male and four female mice of reproductive age to live and reproduce. The results, initially, went as expected. The population growth was exponential with the mice population doubling every 55 days. Just shy of a year into the experiment, population growth slowed dramatically. It was at this point in the experiment that the results began to unfold in a more troubling way.

During this stage in the experiment, which Dr. Calhoun deemed as the Stagnation Phase C, the normal social order and function of the mice began to break down. A large number of adult male mice did not mate or strike out on their own. Instead, these adult male mice began to congregate in an open main area of Mouse Utopia in a socially withdrawn state. In these congregations of mate-less male mice, they exhibited odd psychological and physical inhibitions. So much so that they were later deemed to be "dropouts" by Dr. Calhoun. Though they were congregating in large crowds, they initiated very little social interaction with any other mice. Occasionally, senseless violence among these male mice would break out. Often, the victim would not flee but take the abuse. Scarring could be found on most of these mice. Later on, these previously hurt mice would lash out at other mice.

The other male mice, who were able to mate, began to abandon their roles as protectors of their females and young. The female mice that went without the protection of the male mice went on to be aggressive beyond their normal nature.

Death2 - Our Old, Tired Way

Eventually, these female mice also began to abandon their young. Unthinkably, in the absence of the protection of male mice, females would even take to harming their own young. This would often result in the death of the young. If they survived, many of these abandoned young would become socially unadjusted adults. Socially unadjusted adult females would isolate themselves into corners of Mouse Utopia to live out their days alone.

In the midst of these social disruptions, the birthrate in Mouse Utopia plummeted. Pregnancies became exceedingly rare. Many of these young mice didn't make it beyond being weaned due to the poor mothering. Bizarrely, many of the unadjusted adult males were entirely uninterested in mating. Deemed by Dr. Calhoun as the "Beautiful Ones", they would spend countless hours grooming themselves. Eventually, these adult mice would not function in any normal social behavioral roles beyond simply maintaining their own bodies. Finally, pregnancies no longer occurred. Births stopped entirely. With no social, familial, or reproductive norms being upheld, the population of Mouse Utopia became extinct four years into the experiment. Despite ideal physical conditions for the mice population, they failed to reproduce and all died. They're freedom in utopia led to their demise, not their flourishing.

Mouse Utopia proved to be a dystopian death experiment. In his conclusions regarding his experiment, Dr.

Calhoun remarked about the mice living in the utopia, "Autistic-like creatures, capable only of the most simple behaviors compatible with physiological survival, emerge out of this process. Their spirit has died."[2] The hollowness of the physically easy conditions and the breakdown of normal social roles resulted in death. Their lives were so empty that these mice lost their will to survive. Thankfully, these disturbing revelations are only about simple-minded creatures who are merely rodents, right? But as Dr. Calhoun goes on to say, he considers that this example may have ramifications for humans:

> "For an animal so complex as man, there is no logical reason why a comparable sequence of events should not also lead to species extinction…Individuals born under these circumstances will be so out of touch with reality so as to be incapable of even alienation…Acquisition, creation, and utilization of ideas appropriation for life in a post-industrial cultural-conceptual-technological society will have been blocked."[3]

Friends, why does this experiment from 1973 seem to strike so uncomfortably close to home? Why does the social and behavioral dysfunction observed in mice over 50 years ago seem so familiar? That's because Mouse Utopia has begun to manifest in our world. Mouse Utopia is becoming our reality. Am I proposing that the Fourth Horseman of the Apocalypse is imminently coming? No. But, the world we are living in seems to be looking more and more similar to this dystopian rodent world.

In the abundance of our Western world, we have nearly all of our physical needs met. We have an abundance of food and clean water. We have large, warm homes. Thankfully, we don't have to worry about being eaten by lions or wolves. In a world free from near constant physical threats, we are free to pursue other passions or interests. So we do. Pleasure becomes our highest goal. Incessant entertainment rules us. Our god becomes our stomachs. The virtual has supplanted the actual. Responsibilities are redefined as burdens. Self-satisfaction trumps genuine connection. The result is a people who have much better physical conditions than our ancestors, but a soul condition that is far worse.

Let's contemplate some of the disturbingly similar occurrences happening in our world today. Like the adult males in Mouse Utopia who were able to reproduce, countless men who have children and families are abandoning them. One in three children will grow up in the United States without their biological father.[4] These children, specifically the boys, who are fatherless are less likely to grow up well adjusted to society. These boys are 72% more likely to be idle (not working or in school), 250% less likely to graduate college, and 200% more likely to be incarcerated.[5] The normal, healthy functioning among men has begun to break down.

The Better Way

Consider the large collection of unmated or unproductive male mice gathering in Mouse Utopia. Today, there are entire communities of men that are labeled (sometimes by choice, sometimes by others) "incels." This name "incel" comes from the short hand of "involuntarily celibate" because they believe they're unable to find a woman to be intimate with and live life with.[6] In the greater population, middle-aged and young men's employment participation rates are the lowest in American history.[7] In terms of engaging in real life, 48% of young men say they are more engaged and rewarded by the online world.[8] Among young men aged 18-23, many feel disconnected relationally, with a staggering 65% believing "No one really knows me."[9] Many men in our society struggle with socially adjusting to our world. Eerily similar, isn't it?

Women have not escaped our reality-based reflection of Mouse Utopia unscathed either. In the absence of a father, women are often forced to raise children alone. One in four children live only with their mother in the United States.[10] Tragically and ironically, in the same year (1973) that this study was released, Roe vs Wade gave the greenlight to the elimination of tens of millions of unwanted pregnancies. Human young are being abandoned and attacked by women who are often abandoned by the father and aided by the medical system. Subsequently, birth rates have plummeted across the Western world, including the United States. The number of children born per fertile women has dropped from 3.65 in 1960 to 1.64 in 2020.[11] Men, women, children, and the entire family have begun to reflect what was observed in the initial phases of the "Stagnation Phase C" in Dr. Calhoun's experiment. This is frightening. This ought to be sobering.

I would posit that Dr. Calhoun did not discover anything new about the nature of humanity. Instead, Dr. Calhoun demonstrated, through the overly simplistic lives of rodents, what happens when humanity chooses to go its own way. It is the "second death", or the death of the spirit, that Dr. Calhoun discusses in his scholarly journal article. The end game of this old, tired way of living that humanity has chosen for itself is Mouse Utopia, or our own spiritual death. The proof exists in the fruit of our lives. It manifests in the fruit of our societies and families. It is demonstrated in the deteriorating condition of our souls.

Does this mean our world will go the way of Mouse Utopia? Will we end up like those soulless creatures who are so dissatisfied with life that we don't care enough to engage in life with others? Might we give up on the profoundly important roles given to us by both God and nature? Are we bound to become lonely, hopeless people who float through life living in a form of spiritual death? Does our way of living mean the loss of our souls, our spirits, and our humanity?

The Better Way

It can be, but it does not have to be.

By now you may be thinking, "Wow this is really dark," and "Is this book going to offer any form of hope?". I want to be very frank with you. Without intervention from something or someone beyond us, humanity is doomed. We are a violent, corrupt, and hopeless people. The model of Mouse Utopia being the prophetic image of a humanity following its own way in this world is appropriate. It is good for us to soberly consider the state of humanity.

In order for us to have the clear-headedness to choose a better way, we need to look at how awful and tired our current way of living is. Only when we stop medicating our way through life and distracting our weary souls with superficial things can we begin to realize that a change is needed. There is no good news unless we know the bad news. Here's how the Bible describes humanity's condition:

"No one is righteous— not even one. No one is truly wise; no one is seeking God. All have turned away; all have become useless. No one does good, not a single one." "Their talk is foul, like the stench from an open grave. Their tongues are filled with lies." "Snake venom drips from their lips." "Their mouths are full of cursing and bitterness." "They rush to commit murder. Destruction and misery always follow them. They don't know where to find peace." "They have no fear of God at all." Romans 3:10-18

This assessment of humanity is brutal. It's dark. But if we are honest, how much of this is inaccurate about humanity? How much of it is shown to be false when we sincerely consider the way of living our world has modeled for us? Sadly, this way has become the default for us. It isn't working. We are the "Mouse Utopia". We are headed towards a death of body and a death of spirit. Death twice over. Or in the words of Dr. Calhoun, "Death Squared." There MUST be a better way.

So what is the good news behind all of this bad news? In the face of such gloomy circumstances for us as a people, where can we find hope?

Thankfully, there is a way for humanity through this darkness. The good news is that there is a way for us through this "second death". But in order to do justice to how truly Good the good news is, we need to go back to the beginning. Way back. We need to look at the kind of world we were purposed for, the way of living we were originally created for.

Chapter 2

The Way God Intended

"Then God looked over all he had made, and he saw that it was very good!"
Genesis 1:31

In my childhood there was a place that was greater than Disney World. It was better than a candy store where everything was free. It was even better than any blowout birthday party. It was my favorite place on planet Earth. This fantastical place of my childhood was Nana and Papa's house. Their home felt as if it was literally the destination described in the "over the hills and through the woods" childhood rhyme. It was the closest place to heaven on Earth for me.

My grandparents, affectionately known to me as Nana and Papa, lived just across the border in Northern Wisconsin. They had 16 acres of hills, trees, open space, and a beautiful cabin-like home. On their property was an enormous pole barn filled with tractors, four wheelers, and toys. Well-groomed four wheeling trails stretched throughout their woods. A tubing hill in the winter and a colossal slip-n-slide in the summer lay right outside their front door. Squirrel hunting with BB guns and large bonfires were a regular occurrence. The annual Fourth of July,

The Better Way

homemade fireworks displays have never been beaten by any other shows I've seen.

Inside of their house was nearly as thrilling as outside. The computer room was an entire room dedicated to video games where endless hours of Call of Duty were played. Elsewhere in the house were brand new TVs and new game systems at our disposal. The freezer was always full of ice cream and whipped cream. The basement fridge was never less than half full of pop. Another room in the basement had a wood-burning furnace and was lightheartedly called "Smokey Joe's." In that room, my great-grandfather and grandfather (Papa) would tell me stories of long ago as they smoked their pipes.

One of the highlights of the year was our annual Christmas tradition. Nana and Papa love to give generous gifts, but they would always credit Santa Clause. In order to bolster the tradition, my grandfather would tell us that Santa was running behind so he dropped our presents out of the sleigh as he passed overhead. Our job was to hunt them down in the woods surrounding the house. We would all load up into a wagon pulled by the tractor and "find" the presents Santa dropped for us. After we gathered all of our presents, we would ride back to the house through the snow. There, my grandmother would have hot chocolate and whipped cream ready for us to drink as we opened up our presents together. Like I said, there was no place on Earth more fun for me as a kid.

Why was my grandparents' house such an amazing place? How did all of these fairy-tale like conditions exist in one location? How could a kid have such wonderful memories of a random house in small-town Wisconsin? All of this was possible because of one reason. Nana and Papa intended it to be that way. My grandparents desired to create the most ideal conditions for their grandchildren to enjoy life and make wonderful memories with them. It worked!

This precious picture of loving grandparents intentionally designing their home to provide their grandchildren with idyllic conditions reflects what our Creator designed for us. At the very beginning of human history, God created perfect conditions for humanity. Before humanity even breathed its first breath, God was busy preparing a place for us to live. Inside of this wonderful place, He was structuring a way of living for us that was ideal. This place and way of living was full of pleasure, full of intimacy, and full of life.

God, in his great affection for humanity, gave us a way of living that was wildly good. Obviously, this is not how our world looks now. Things have changed much since our creation, which we will discuss in the next two chapters. For now, let's reflect on the original design for our way of life as humans.

> *"So God created human beings in his own image. In the image of God he created them; male and female he created them. Then God blessed them and said, "Be fruitful and multiply. Fill the earth and govern it. Reign over the fish in the sea, the birds in the sky, and all the animals that scurry along the ground."* Genesis 1:27-28

In these opening sentences about humanity, there are an entire host of conclusions that we can draw from what the Bible says about how God created us. All of those conclusions are exceedingly good!

Firstly, we were created with a perfect template. God chose to create us in His image. Though we are merely created beings in comparison to our creator, we certainly do reflect some of His attributes. In His image, we have a great capacity to love. Humanity was built with compassion and a nurturing heart. In His image, we have the ability to choose. We are given free will and agency. In His image, we thirst for justice. We long for everyone to get what they are rightfully due. In His image, we desire intimate relationship and to be known. God longed for us to know Him and for Him to know us. This was the way we were meant to live.

Secondly, humanity was created with the ability to create life! We were told to, *"be fruitful and multiply."* This is true in a couple of ways. One being the very reproductive nature weaved into our DNA as male and female. God gave a charge to humans to reproduce and create life. He intended for our way of life to be fruitful and multiplicative. Another way we are creators is demonstrated through how we have become inventors, innovators, artists, musicians, poets, gardeners, merchants, educators, and so on. In our purest form, a creative capacity follows us in all that we do. God's design for us was to be a fruitful, creative, and multiplying people. Life and creativity were meant to be natural outflows from our lives. This is the way we were meant to live.

Thirdly, like God reigns and governs the entire universe, so were we given the right to reign and govern the Earth. Verse 28 says, *"...Fill the earth and govern it. Reign over the fish in the sea, the birds in the sky, and all the animals that scurry along the ground."* The Earth was meant to be our playground, our great adventure, and our opportunity to reflect God's image in us. Reigning and governing, taming and subduing do not bring destruction but flourishing. God's original intention for our way of life was to be about governing, reigning, and bringing order to things. We were given a meaningful role in governing the Earth so that creation flourished. This is the way we were meant to live.

Entire books could be written on these beautiful aspects of God's design for humans demonstrated in Genesis 1. For the sake of brevity, we will leave it there and look at the more detailed account of man and woman being created in Genesis 2.

The Better Way

> *"Then the Lord God formed the man from the dust of the ground. He breathed the breath of life into the man's nostrils, and the man became a living person. Then the Lord God planted a garden in Eden in the east, and there he placed the man he had made. The Lord God made all sorts of trees grow up from the ground—trees that were beautiful and that produced delicious fruit. In the middle of the garden he placed the tree of life and the tree of the knowledge of good and evil."* Genesis 2:7-9

Want to talk about fullness of life? How about the Creator of the universe breathing life straight into you! A breath from God filling our lungs and giving us the capacity to live! Our first interaction with existence was with the author of life itself. Genesis 3 describes a pattern where mankind would walk daily with God. This was mankind's original position with our Creator, intimacy and deep relationship with Him. We were meant to live intimately knowing God.

God was also purposeful in where He placed us to begin life. Verse 8 says, *"Then the Lord God planted a garden in Eden in the east, and there he placed the man he had made."* God gave us everything we need for life in the Garden of Eden and put us in it! A beautiful home. Endless food. Productive land. Delicious fruit. Probably, lots of carbohydrates and sugar at our fingertips. Pleasure, abundance, and beauty were a part of God's original intention for humanity. We were meant to live in the abundance of God's creation.

The Way God Intended

What stands out most pointedly about the Garden of Eden is what is placed at the center of it. Two trees. Verse 9 says, *"...In the middle of the garden he placed the tree of life and the tree of the knowledge of good and evil."* The first tree is the "tree of life". Eating of this tree gave us access to life, eternal life. A gift from God. Death had no part of this original plan God had for humanity. We were meant to live a life with no end.

The second tree was "the tree of the knowledge of good and evil". We later find out that eating of this tree would bring death. So why was it in the middle of the Garden of Eden? It demonstrates that humanity has a capacity for choice. The choice was presented to us to either eat of the tree that God forbade or to abstain from it. We were given agency. In our original design, we were given a choice by God to remain in this place of life with Him or enter into our own way, the way of death. We were meant to live with agency and free will.

> *"18 Then the Lord God said, 'It is not good for the man to be alone. I will make a helper who is just right for him'... 22 Then the Lord God made a woman from the rib, and he brought her to the man... 25 Now the man and his wife were both naked, but they felt no shame."* Genesis 2:18;22;25

Finally, we get to one of the best parts! Verse 25 says, *"Now the man and his wife were both naked..."*. Romance, intimacy,

The Better Way

and sex. Yes, even sex had its place in God's original design. This romantic and sexual part of our nature was bound up inside of a beautiful intimacy intended to exist in a life-surrendering relationship between a man and a woman. Full trust, full vulnerability, and a pure desire to bring the other pleasure.

Even non-romantic relationships more broadly have tremendous meaning for us as we look at God's intended way of living for humanity. We were created to have deep relationships with each other. Loneliness is not good! God explicitly said in verse 18, "...*It is not good for man to be alone...*" so He gave us each other. Isolation is outside of God's original plan. Intimacy, friendship, and community are deeply integrated into God's design of humanity.

Amazingly, there was no shame in God's original design. Verse 25 goes on to say, "...*but they felt no shame.*" We were never meant to live in shame. We were never intended to live in regret. Sorrow, remorse, guilt, and self-condemnation are not anywhere in God's original design for us. We were never meant to live that way. Instead, innocence and purity were our birthrights.

If we consider all of these objectively good things in God's original design for us, what does it mean? If we take everything God sowed into us as His creation, what are we to think of Him? In short, God designed humanity to flourish. God, from the very beginning, has always intended for humanity to

The Way God Intended

live a full life. It also means that God desires to be Good to us. Anger, judgment, and discipline were not originally a part of God's purposes towards humanity. Only blessing and love were. Just like I know my grandparents always loved me by the conditions they created for me at their blissful Wisconsin home, we too can know the nature of God in how He created such wonderful conditions for us to live in. God loves humanity and desires life for us. It's the way we were meant to live.

This all sounds so good! We had everything we could ever want or need in the original design of humanity. The way God intended for us to live in our beginnings is the best way. Unfortunately, this is no longer our reality.

How did our beautiful creation story turn into something resembling Mouse Utopia today? How did we fall so far from this wonderful description of how God lovingly intended for us to live?

We decided to choose our own way instead.

Chapter 3

The Way of Corruption

"Since they thought it foolish to acknowledge God, he abandoned them to their foolish thinking and let them do things that should never be done."
Romans 1:28

The spring that my oldest son turned three years old, my wife and I made a weighty decision. Our decision would deeply affect how our sons experienced the approaching summer and many summers to come. Maybe even how they remembered their early childhood. It was time to act. We decided to install a swing set in our backyard.

Since my wife and I were trying to be thrifty, we decided to disassemble, move, and reassemble an old swing set we found online from a nice home on the other side of our town. That evening, for two very cold hours in the Iowa wind, a friend and I worked vigorously to disassemble a swing set. Very quickly, I realized that the swing set was going to be a bigger job than I had anticipated. Not only did it fill the entire back of our minivan, but its condition was worse than we had expected. This swing set, being used, had endured many seasons in our Midwestern climate. It had not weathered well. Many of the boards had begun to rot out. The corruption and decay of our climate had set in.

After bringing the swing set home, I awoke early the next morning to begin the re-assembling process in our backyard. Our oldest son, Winston, was eager to see what I was doing. That morning he sat outside for hours in the cold with great anticipation as a tired, old swing set began to take shape in front of him. After assembling everything on the set that wasn't rotten, I evaluated its condition. It was ROUGH. Nearly all of the ground-level boards were unusable. The supporting posts were compromised structurally. If we were going to keep this swing set, new wood was needed to reinforce it and the entire set would have to be stained. There were probably 12-15 more hours of work and hundreds of dollars left to be spent. Even then, the final product would not be pretty. It would be a Frankenstein swing set.

After talking it over with my wife, we decided to tear down the entire set (again) and bring it to the dump. Winston began to weep as I tore down this broken, rotted out swing set and loaded it back into our van. A few days later, a new swing set that we ordered online arrived at our house. It was smaller and not as extravagant as the old swing set, but it would be structurally sound. Our son joyfully received his early birthday present after I assembled the new set a week later.

The Way of Corruption

Through the many grueling hours of work that I sacrificed for my sons, I was left with one central observation, the tremendous damage that is caused by corruption. Here was a shocking reality I considered as I was driving to the dump: that old swing set was once brand new. The boards stabilizing the structure had been solid. The wood once looked fresh. Kids could jump, swing, slide, and climb all over that swing set without it falling over or pieces snapping off. Until rot and the corruption of the elements set in, it was a usable and wonderful swing set.

Oddly, this rotten, corrupted swing set is emblematic of the state humanity finds itself in. In many ways, it is representative of us all. The reality and way of living that we were created to experience with God in the beginning no longer exists. Instead, this world of corruption has taken its place. Decay has taken the place of perfection. How did this happen? Where did we go wrong as a people?

In the Bible passage immediately following the description of God's intended way for humanity, we see where the departure from it occurs. Here is a glimpse into the moment where humanity chose its own way and the effect of corruption that took place as a result:

The Better Way

> *"The serpent was the shrewdest of all the wild animals the Lord God had made. One day he asked the woman, 'Did God really say you must not eat the fruit from any of the trees in the garden?'*
> *'Of course we may eat fruit from the trees in the garden,' the woman replied. 'It's only the fruit from the tree in the middle of the garden that we are not allowed to eat. God said, 'You must not eat it or even touch it; if you do, you will die.''*
> *'You won't die!' the serpent replied to the woman. 'God knows that your eyes will be opened as soon as you eat it, and you will be like God, knowing both good and evil.'"* Genesis 3:1-5

A serpent, which the Bible describes elsewhere as the accuser or devil, shows up on the scene. The serpent quizzes Eve, the first woman, on the rules of living in the garden with God. The rules were pretty straightforward. She knew the boundaries well. They were not to eat of the tree in the middle of the garden, also known as the "tree of the knowledge of good and evil." That's it! They could eat of anything in the entirety of the garden except that singular tree. In the middle of this beautiful simplicity, humanity had a choice. Humanity could reject the lies of this deceiver who was making slanderous claims about God's character. Or, humanity could accept the lie that God can't be trusted, that His ways aren't better, and choose our own way. Which way do you think we chose?

> *"The woman was convinced. She saw that the tree was beautiful and its fruit looked delicious, and she wanted the wisdom it would give*

The Way of Corruption

her. So she took some of the fruit and ate it. Then she gave some to her husband, who was with her, and he ate it, too. At that moment their eyes were opened, and they suddenly felt shame at their nakedness. So they sewed fig leaves together to cover themselves. When the cool evening breezes were blowing, the man and his wife heard the Lord God walking about in the garden. So they hid from the Lord God among the trees. Then the Lord God called to the man, 'Where are you?' He replied, 'I heard you walking in the garden, so I hid. I was afraid because I was naked.'" Genesis 3:6-10

There it is. The moment that changed everything. This was the moment that humanity decided to go its own way. The way of corruption entered into our world and the human race. Just like that old swing set that was once free of decay and operating as it was designed to, our corruption has deviated us from God's design. The only difference is that we invited the corruption in. We chose it. We believed the lie.

This begs the question of each one of us now, in our moment of history. Have you and I believed the same lie? Have we believed that God, if we have decided there is one, is not to be trusted? Do we believe in a Good God or the lies of a serpent? Questioning God's intentions and purposes caused us to fall off the cliff into our own decay and spiritual death. In our questioning of His goodness towards us and rejection of His way, we have begun down the journey of corruption.

The magnitude of humanity's decision cannot be overstated. This is how sin, evil, and death entered into the world. Many ask the question, "How can a Good God allow evil in our world?" The answer is short. We chose it. Humanity decided that God's way wasn't best. We turned away from an ideal, perfect life with an exceedingly Good God to go our own way. And any way that isn't God's way is corrupt and eventually leads to death.

But why would God allow humanity to turn away from Him? Why would He give us the choice? Didn't He know we would choose our own way? Is He some sick being that enjoys seeing His creation suffer?

These very questions demonstrate how we don't trust the Goodness of God. Ever since humanity's choice to turn to its own way, we've continued to struggle to believe He is who He says He is. I believe the answer to those questions comes from the Good nature of God. The Bible describes love in 1 Corinthians 13:5 by saying, *"It does not demand its own way."* God, as an abundantly loving God, did not demand His own way in us. Why else would the only tree that caused death be located in the middle of the garden? He did not demand His own way. Instead, He let us, in His love, freely choose. This richly loving and faithful God allowed us to go our own way. In His love towards us, He allowed us not to choose His way.

The Way of Corruption

Immediately after choosing our own way, we began to feel the effects of corruption that we invited in. Before we even see the word "sin" appear in Genesis 4, "shame" enters the picture. We felt shame before we knew the word sin. Genesis 3:7 says, *"...their eyes were opened, and they suddenly felt shame in their own nakedness."* Shame didn't exist prior to departing from God's way. Only in our way did we begin to experience shame. Feeling guilty, feeling shame, and feeling self-condemnation are the immediate results of choosing our own way.

In their shame, humanity cut itself off from God. In verses 8-10, the man and woman hid from God. Their own shame distanced them from God. God, who certainly knew what had taken place, called out saying, "Where are you?" These humans, who God had breathed life itself into, replied back that they were afraid. Fear had entered into the human experience. In the very first moments of humanity choosing its own way, we experienced shame and fear. This was never a part of the way God intended for us.

As the story of humanity goes on in Genesis 3 and 4, we see even more consequences from this choice. Sin, which is choosing anything that isn't God's best for us, always brings along a curse. The curse of pain was released onto humanity. The Earth was cursed by humanity. The curse of death was given power over humanity. As it says in Genesis 3:19, *"...For you were made from dust, and to dust you will return."* The causal factor of our own spiritual and physical death is not a gleefully twisted Creator but the product of our own choices. God's perfect justice demands a penalty for every evil action. Thus, we experience the penalty for sin when we choose our own way.

Eventually, humanity began to commit more and more heinous sins. What started as eating a forbidden fruit in Genesis 3 turned into full-fledged murder between brothers in Genesis 4. Humanity launched into a wild, scary journey down its own way, even as God continued to warn us of the consequences.

Again, God let humanity go down our own dark road that we chose. In the book of Romans, the first chapter describes humanity's ever more evil ways.

"Since they thought it foolish to acknowledge God, he abandoned them to their foolish thinking and let them do things that should never be done. Their lives became full of every kind of wickedness, sin, greed, hate, envy, murder, quarreling, deception, malicious behavior, and gossip. They are backstabbers, haters of God, insolent, proud, and boastful. They invent new ways of sinning, and they disobey their parents. They refuse to understand, break their promises, are heartless, and have no mercy. They know God's justice requires that those who do these things deserve to die, yet they do them anyway. Worse yet, they encourage others to do them, too." Romans 1:28-32

The Way of Corruption

This passage, while pretty damning about humanity's errors, is very revealing about our world today. All the evil. All the suffering. All the pain. It all comes as a by-product of the sin that we willingly opened the door to.

God allowed us to "get what we deserve and get it good and hard." Some may claim that this isn't loving. Some may claim that this isn't what a Good God would do. But what good father would always protect his children from every possible consequence of their actions? Instead, He has allowed us to feel our own consequences. It is God's mercy that allows us to feel guilty and ashamed when we depart from His way. He let us feel the pain that comes from our own way so that we may see how truly Good His way is!

Remarkably, in the middle of listing off the consequences of sin to Adam and Eve in Genesis 3, God already begins to build a way out. In verse 15, God references one who would come through the line of Eve that would "crush" the head of the serpent. The deceiver, who helped initiate mankind's fall, would ultimately be crushed. This whisper of hope in one of the darkest moments of history displays God's Good desire to provide a way out for us. Even though we rightfully deserve the repercussions that come with choosing our own way, God longs to redeem humanity. He plans to bring a better way to us again.

Chapter 4

The Way of Religion

"For no one can ever be made right with God by doing what the law commands. The law simply shows us how sinful we are."
Romans 3:20

Ever since I graduated high school, working out has become one of my favorite hobbies. Originally, I was a runner. After I ran a marathon at the end of my college career, I wanted a new challenge. That challenge came in the form of a high-intensity interval training regime called CrossFit. Yes, I am one of those people, but it has become a daily activity for our family. After buying a new home, my wife and I decided to turn our garage into a CrossFit gym. It has given us sustainable and easy access to a life of fitness. With children, our gym has become a room where they see "mommy and daddy" work hard, sweat, and challenge themselves. Consequently, our kids get to be around and grow familiar with pullup bars, dumbbells, barbells, and other items found in a CrossFit gym.

One day, when my oldest son wasn't quite three years old, my workout included sets of moderately heavy deadlifts. A dead lift is a motion with a barbell and weight plates where you lift the bar from ground level to about waist level. It's a simple movement that allows you to really load up the bar with weight. At the end of the workout, my barbell was safely sitting on the floor with over 200 lbs of weight still loaded onto it. My then two-year-old son, wanting to do what "daddy" does, walked up to the barbell. He placed his hands tightly around the bar and lifted with all of his might. Incredibly, he lifted the entire bar off the ground!

Just kidding. My son handled the 200+ lb barbell in the exact way you would expect any two-year-old to handle it. The bar didn't budge. Despite the many grunts and extreme amount of effort put forward by this tenacious toddler, the weight would not move. It was an impossible task for him. A toddler cannot lift hundreds of pounds off the floor. While being an adorable kid, there was no way he could ever lift the bar on his own.

When humanity fell into trouble by choosing its own way, we found ourselves in a similarly impossible situation. Even with the clearheadedness to recognize the trajectory of our path, we couldn't change our way of living if we tried. Attempting to get off our road headed towards corruption through our own effort is just as impossible. It's just as infeasible of an undertaking as a toddler attempting to lift a barbell weighing hundreds of pounds. It cannot be done. We are wholly unable to get off our own way headed to destruction regardless of how hard we try.

The Way of Religion

Despite this impossibility, this is an attempt that humanity has made over and over again. Many of us are aware of the brokenness of humanity and are desperate to fix it. This is why our world has so many religions. This is why moral codes are often instituted across societies. Yet, none of our efforts can do anything to alter our tragic state. When humanity turned to its own way by eating of the forbidden fruit, a permanent mark was left upon us. A corruption was invited into our lives that cannot be uninvited or rid of. Our trajectory towards decay and death is firmly fixed. Throughout large portions of the Old Testament (the first ¾ of the Bible) we see humans make attempt after attempt trying to fix their own way. Each time failing. Each time falling short.

During the time of Moses, a code of conduct, or the Law, was given to the Israelite people.[12] As the nation that God wanted to display His goodness to all of humanity through, the Israelites were given the Law as an inherent good. It was meant to show humanity God's Way for us. It was meant to bless us.

"Study this Book of Instruction continually. Meditate on it day and night so you will be sure to obey everything written in it. Only then will you prosper and succeed in all you do." Joshua 1:8

While this passage is specifically addressed to the leader of the Israelites named Joshua, its meaning is true for all people. The "Book of Instruction", or Law, is good for us. It is the standard that God expects for people who want to live according to His ways. In following His Law, there would be blessing and fruitfulness. In choosing our own way, we would continue in our decay and corruption.

In having the Law, the Israelites demonstrated one significant truth. Humans can NEVER live up to the standard that God has set. All of God's chosen people in the Old Testament failed to live up to God's ways. The Law couldn't be upheld by the kings, the priests, or even the prophets. Every single human that has attempted to return back to God's way for us in the Garden by following the Law could not do it. It's a standard far too high for us to reach. It's a weight far too heavy for us to lift. It cannot be done on our own. Restoration back to God through the Law is impossible.

> *"For no one can ever be made right with God by doing what the law commands. The law simply shows us how sinful we are… For everyone has sinned; we all fall short of God's glorious standard."*
> Romans 3:20,23

The Bible explicitly tells us we cannot meet God's standard. God's ways are perfect and so His standard is perfect. Therefore, we can never live up to it. Yet, we still often try to.

The Way of Religion

Humanity's tendency to try to work its way back to God is never ending. We are desperate to prove that we can get back to Him and His way for us. People of every type do this at some level. Whether we are trying to get to heaven, be a good person, or be restored to God's ways, we all measure ourselves according to our moral or religious efforts.

I often call this the "Scoreboard Mentality". Each one of us subconsciously believes there is an enormous scoreboard in the sky keeping track of our rights and our wrongs. If we do things that are morally right, we get points. We think that going to church, participating in the right social media trends, donating to a good cause, or paying someone a compliment will win us points in heaven or prove we are a good person. The opposite is true of how we view our wrongs. If we don't go to church, swear at a person in traffic, or ignore those heart-wrenching commercials asking for our money, then we lose points.

In this mentality, we believe that the score on the scoreboard at the end of our life is what we are judged by. If the score is above 0 at the end of our life, then we get to heaven or we have proved we are a good person. If we end our lives with the scoreboard below 0, then we go to hell or we are judged as a bad person.

The Better Way

Even though this "Scoreboard Mentality" is an unhealthy trap, it actually assumes far too much of our ability to change the outcome of our lives. An accurate scoreboard measuring our lives would be infinitely negative. Our scoreboard would always read less than 0. We cannot add enough points to ever change the score. Choosing our own way is a hole that we can never get out of by our own works. Our moral efforts and religious fervor are futile.

God knew that our religious and moral efforts would amount to nothing. He has accurately assessed our tragic condition. He knows that we can never escape the consequences of choosing our own way. Seeing humanity in such a disastrous state, God had compassion on us. Because of His compassion, God decided to make a way where there was no way. At a great cost to Himself, He gave us The Way.

Chapter 5

The Way

"Jesus told him, 'I am the way, the truth, and the life. No one can come to the Father except through me.'" John 14:6

In the very first months of working my job as an environmental engineer in the Minneapolis metro area, I became intimately familiar with the harshness of life that our world can bring. It was a dark and bitterly cold morning in December as I was nearing the end of my 45-minute commute. About two miles away from work, my 2002 Volkswagen Cabrio began to experience trouble. BEEP. BEEP. BEEP. Not only was the check engine light on, but it was flashing red! Immediately, I pulled over and began to research what all the alarms and lights meant. It turned out that my engine was low on oil. Luckily, I had an extra quart of oil in my trunk. After pouring the quart of oil into the engine and starting the car again, the alarms and lights stopped. I was able to make it the rest of the way to work.

Once I arrived at work, I started to feel pretty sick. Around 10 AM in the morning, my stomach was churning, and I felt nauseous. Two hours later my mouth began to water, and whatever was in my stomach violently surged up. I vomited into my office's trash can. It was a low moment. After telling my boss

The Better Way

that I had just puked, I got my stuff and made my way to the car. I was going to ride out whatever this sickness was at home in my warm, cozy bed. After I loaded my stuff in my car, I started the engine to drive home.

Within 30 seconds of driving down the road, it happened again. BEEP. BEEP. BEEP. Red flashing lights. I decided to push my luck and drive an extra mile to a gas station to buy more oil. After pouring the new oil into my engine, the lights did not turn off and the beeping continued. I looked underneath my car, and oil was pooling on the ground as it poured out the bottom of my engine. My car had an oil leak, and I would certainly ruin the engine if I drove home. About that time, I began to feel sick again. I hurried into the gas station bathroom. Right when I reached the toilet, I began to vomit. On my hands and knees puking into a gas station toilet with a car broken down outside, I realized I was in trouble. There was no way home for me. It was a low moment.

Thankfully, I did what most people do when they have car trouble. I called my dad. Upon hearing of my desperate condition, he dropped everything at his work to drive over an hour to pick me up. He drove me home as I was lying in the back seat trying not to vomit. After making sure I was comfortable at home, he called the shop that had just worked on my car a few days prior. He haggled with them over the phone and demanded they fix their poor work. The shop paid for my tow across the city and fixed the oil leak free of charge. Within two days, I was feeling better and my car was no longer leaking oil. It was quite the turnaround!

That situation made me so grateful for my dad. When I was at my lowest moment, puking into a gas station toilet with a broken-down car, he came to my aid. I was in no condition to find a ride for myself or to get my car to a mechanic. At a sacrifice to his own schedule and priorities, he came to my help. He rescued me from my dire situation and did for me what I could not do for myself.

Likewise, this is the situation humanity finds itself in. Our circumstances are bleak. Our own way has brought us into a place of pain and desperation. In choosing our own way, we have put ourselves into a position where we are incapable of helping ourselves. Thankfully, God, who chooses to take the role of our loving Father, has decided to come to our aid. He decided to do for us what we could not do for ourselves. He has provided a way out for us.

God's way out for humanity didn't take the shape or form that many would have expected. Many may have expected a violent explosion of God's power to be demonstrated across the sky. Many may have expected a political revolution that instituted a religious governmental authority that demanded humanity change by the threat of force. Instead, God's plan for the salvation of humanity was more subtle. It took on a form that would have shocked the people at the time and still shocks people today. Just because God's method was different than we would potentially expect, that doesn't mean it wasn't adequate. It was more than adequate. It was the exact solution humanity needed. And as with anything God does, it is better than we think.

What was God's perfect plan for humanity's redemption? A child named Jesus.

God sent His own Son, Jesus, to provide the way out for humanity. Coming to serve humanity, He took on the lowly position of a baby. He was not born to a queen in a palace but to a young woman in a stable meant for animals. Being the Son of God, Jesus grew as a man, both divine and human. Jesus's humanity means He lived life like us. He uniquely understands our pain, our suffering, and what it's like to be human. His divinity allowed Him to live a perfect, sinless life. Jesus lived out His life the way God had intended for all of humanity to live. Since we had chosen the way of corruption and could not escape it, Jesus had to come to do what no man or woman could ever do.

Jesus showed us the way we were meant to live as He yielded his life to His Father, God. He followed God's Law completely. Unfortunately, only demonstrating God's way wasn't enough. Our corruption was too powerful. The consequences for our sin were too great. Jesus had to do something more to take care of the power that sin and corruption held over humanity. Jesus had to do something unbelievable to pay the price and take on the consequences for that corruption. So Jesus did the unfathomable. Brutally and humiliatingly, Jesus accepted an undeserved punishment. His own countrymen nailed Him to a wooden cross to die like a common criminal. Jesus, God in the flesh, gave up His life for us.

"Though he was God, he did not think of equality with God as something to cling to. Instead, he gave up his divine privileges; he took the humble position of a slave and was born as a human being. When he appeared in human form, he humbled himself in obedience to God and died a criminal's death on a cross." Philippians 2:6-8

Jesus's precious life was sinless. Jesus's precious life was perfect. Jesus's life demonstrated His power and divinity. Yet, to take on the consequences of corruption caused by humanity's dark ways, He chose to give up His life. He took the consequences of our rebellion so we didn't have to. Jesus gave up His life to break the power of sin and corruption in our life. He broke its power because we would never be able to. His death means our chance at life.

All of this is a demonstration of God's great love for humanity. God greatly desires to redeem us from the way of corruption. Romans 5:8 says, *"But God showed his great love for us by sending Christ to die for us while we were still sinners."*

The death of Jesus catalyzed much. It was a great work that accomplished a great deal. But God did not let Jesus remain in death. By the power of God, Jesus was raised back to life. Though He experienced death, Jesus emerged from the tomb victorious over corruption and the death it wrought.

Jesus, who accomplished humanity's release from the consequences of sin and corruption through His death, accomplished even more through His resurrection. His resurrection accomplishes the work of restoring humanity back to the life we were meant to live with God from the beginning. His resurrection showed that God's plan for redeeming humanity from the way that leads to death worked. Now, we have a way back to God's original purpose for humanity. Jesus is that way.

"Jesus told him, 'I am the way, the truth, and the life. No one can come to the Father except through me.'" John 14:6

No amount of hard work will bring us back to God. No amount of religious practice will earn our spot with God in the Garden again. There is no other way back to what God intended for us other than through Jesus. Jesus is our way to experience the life we were meant to live again.

The Way

If we want life, we have to choose Jesus as our way.

This is the part about the way of Jesus that trips people up the most. He is the ONLY way to life, and we must choose Him.

Jesus is both wildly inclusive in His invitation to all and wildly exclusive in being the only way. All are invited to follow Jesus. No race, no language, no nationality, no gender, and no age has exclusive rights to Jesus. 1 Timothy 2:3-4 says, *"This is good, and pleases God our Savior, who wants all people to be saved and to come to a knowledge of the truth."* God wants all people to choose Jesus! But that doesn't mean all people will. Jesus is exclusive in being the only way. No other religion. No other god. No other means by which we might be saved. Jesus is the only way.

The Way of Jesus is our choice alone. God's desire to love us through Jesus is the same as it was when He created us in the Garden of Eden. He will not force His own way on us. Choosing Jesus is a choice we get to make. The choice between the Tree of Life or the Tree of the Knowledge of Good and Evil still exists. We can choose our own way or the WAY.

Choosing the way of Jesus is a decision you alone have to make. No one else can make it for you. God certainly won't. In His great love for you, God longs for you to choose Him. But

The Better Way

He won't force you. We, ourselves, have to actively make the decision to follow Him into His ways.

In one of the last messages the great prophet Moses gave to the Israelite people, he presented them with a choice. To live life according to God's ways or to choose their own way. As we talked about in the prior chapter, the people of Israel failed to choose God because they could not live up to His standard. This is why Jesus had to come to be the Way for us. Thousands of years later, in light of Jesus offering His life to be the way back to God, it still serves a distinct call for us to make our own choice:

> *"Today I have given you the choice between life and death, between blessings and curses. Now I call on heaven and earth to witness the choice you make. Oh, that you would choose life, so that you and your descendants might live! You can make this choice by loving the Lord your God, obeying him, and committing yourself firmly to him. This is the key to your life…"* Deuteronomy 30:19-20

This is about as clear as it gets. Choose God's way (Jesus) and live. Choose your own way and die. This seems as obvious as choosing to get in the car with my dad to go home after spending the afternoon vomiting into a gas station toilet. Who would want to stay stranded in that dirty gas station with the flu? Similarly, who wouldn't choose life? Who wouldn't want to experience life as God intended? Why wouldn't we want Jesus to take on the spiritual consequences of our sinfulness and corruption?

Choosing God's way means saying "no" to our own way. As we will discuss more in the next chapter, this is hard for all of us. We tend to like our own way. We've grown comfortable with it. But Jesus Himself presents the choice like this:

"You can enter God's Kingdom only through the narrow gate. The highway to hell is broad, and its gate is wide for the many who choose that way. But the gateway to life is very narrow and the road is difficult, and only a few ever find it" Matthew 7:13-14

My hope and prayer is that we all choose this narrow gate. Though the narrow gate of following Jesus is difficult and appears to be costly, it is the only one that leads to life. May we be ones who choose that narrow way!

Chapter 6

The Way of the Cross

"Then Jesus said to his disciples, 'If any of you wants to be my follower, you must give up your own way, take up your cross, and follow me.'"
Matthew 16:24

    Every good love story has a beginning. For my wife and I, that beginning was the first Chi Alpha Campus Ministry gathering of our sophomore year in college. Our relationship began and remained a genuine friendship for the remainder of our college careers. About one year after we graduated, we began dating. Getting her to say "yes" to a first date is a thrilling story that I will have to share another time. So much about our relationship was exciting and surprising in how good it proved to be. Very quickly, I realized that our relationship was getting serious. Marriage was a very real possibility to this wonderful woman.

    A couple of months into dating, I was telling Katie about my cousins who were moving to Egypt. Surprisingly, she also had cousins moving to Egypt at nearly the exact same time. Thankfully, our cousins were NOT the same people. My wife and I are unrelated! It was entirely coincidental. This fact had substantial relevance, however, since I had promised my cousin that I was going to visit him after his arrival to his new country. At the same time, Katie's cousins had always said that she was welcome to visit if she made her way over to their side of the world. I couldn't help but suggest that we take a trip to Egypt together. After a few months of persuading Katie, I convinced her to board a plane with me headed towards Cairo, Egypt to visit our cousins. I recognized that the likelihood of being in an exotic place with some of our favorite people on Earth was probably not going to happen again. Even more uniquely, it was the perfect opportunity to ask for her hand in marriage.

In the weeks leading up to our trip, I hurriedly prepared everything needed to make this happen. Katie's father gave me his blessing. The ring that I had ordered arrived. I tricked Katie into getting her nails done with another friend who was about to get engaged. My cousins were busily coordinating everything that would need to be done the day of the proposal to get us to where we needed to be. Lastly, Katie's cousins scoped out a perfect spot for me to propose. The site was going to be the Churchill Gardens at the Mena House Hotel located near the base of the pyramids. My opportunity to put a ring on the finger of my beloved, future wife was going to take place in the shadow of the Great Pyramid of Giza.

Thankfully, our flights from Chicago to Cairo went smoothly. Somehow, I was able to get a ring through Egyptian customs without Katie seeing or security attempting to pull it out of my bag. About five days into our trip, the moment came for us to go to the hotel. Nervously and with great excitement, we crafted the perfect opportunity for Katie and I to be alone in the beautiful

Egyptian gardens. After I had pulled her away to be alone with me, I went down on one knee and told her that I was ready to commit my life to her. With the ring in my hand, I asked if she would be willing to become my wife. And with a loud and emphatic shout she said, "YES!" It was one of the greatest moments of my entire life. Never could I have anticipated our story playing out that way in that foreign place, but I am so very grateful for it.

That moment, however, isn't the end of our story. It was the beginning. That moment where I committed to be her husband was the start of something entirely new. The verbal commitment I made to her that day was later made official by our marriage, and we started an entirely new life together. The "I" of me living as an individual was coming to an end. The "we" of us as a man and woman committing our lives to one another was beginning. In order for me to step into marriage, the "me" had to become "we." A piece of my individuality died so that I could experience something new and beautiful in the union with my wife. It was costly for me to give up that form of my individual existence, but marriage is certainly better!

In much the same way, this is how it looks for each of us who choose to say "yes" to Jesus. When we accept Jesus's invitation to become our way back to God, it's a free gift. We don't have to work for it or earn it. But Jesus's invitation does involve an exchange. Jesus' invitation involves exchanging our old way of living for His. Choosing Jesus means giving up the way and form of our old life and taking on Jesus's way. We exchange our own way for the Better Way.

Even though it's simple to understand in concept, this exchange is no small thing in how it will affect our lives. Surrendering our life and way of living for Jesus's life and His way of living has far-reaching consequences for us. The place that Jesus points to in describing how significant this change will be is to a place He Himself has been. Jesus points us to the cross.

The cross, which was the means by which Jesus's physical life was laid down for humanity, has become the symbol of our exchanged lives. The cross is the place where the consequences for our corruption were put onto Jesus. The cross is the place where God's righteous judgment meant for us was poured out onto Jesus. The cross is where our curse of sin and death was placed upon Jesus, though He was without sin. Like a husband or wife takes on the debts of their new spouse, Jesus took on our debts and bondages.

Not only is this the place where Jesus takes on our lives, but it is also the place where we take on His life. The cross is where Jesus's sinless life, in the eyes of God, is given to us. The cross is where the intimate relationship Jesus had with God the Father was delivered to us. The cross is where the eternal life Jesus experienced was handed over to us. The cross is our salvation from our old, tired way! But, if we want to experience this great exchange, we must do one important thing. We must go to the cross ourselves.

The Way of the Cross

Our own lives need to be given over to Jesus so that we might be given the life of Jesus.

> *"Then Jesus said to his disciples, "If any of you wants to be my follower, you must give up your own way, take up your cross, and follow me. If you try to hang on to your life, you will lose it. But if you give up your life for my sake, you will save it."* Matthew 16:24-25

In order for Jesus to become the way to the Father for us, He had to go to the cross. In order for Jesus to become the way to the Father for us, we also have to go to the cross. We must give up our own way. But, in this costly act of laying down our own lives, we actually find life in Him!

What does this mean for us? How do we pick up our cross and follow Him?

No, this does not mean physically taking metal stakes and nailing them through our hands into a tree. Instead of physical death, Jesus is asking us to bring our way of living to the cross. He is asking us to bring the lesser things of this world that we love and submit them to the cross. He is asking us to bring our ability to be the ruler of our own lives to the cross. In exchange, we take on His way of living. He gives us new things to love. He becomes the one who directs our lives, not us. The "me" in our life turns into "He". It's His life and His ways that we now partake in, not our own. We have the choice to hold onto our old life. We don't have to let it go, but we will miss out on the better life He wants to give us.

Many people have considered the better way offered by Jesus. They've taken account of the fruit of their lives and decided that it was not good. They've looked at the life that Jesus offered and decided that it was better. But when the time came for the laying down of their old life, they found it too difficult. Jesus speaks directly to this temptation in Matthew 16:26, *"And what do you benefit if you gain the whole world but lose your own soul? Is anything worth more than your soul?"* It may be difficult. It may be costly. But it's certainly not more costly than losing our own soul!

In deciding whether the costs of giving up our own way are too great or not, our soul is at stake. Life itself, the one we were made for, hangs in the balance. Our old, tired way will lead to the death of our own soul and spirit. The brokenness of our current world clearly shows the trajectory of that distinctly human way of living. But it is in taking the road that leads to our cross that we actually find life. A whole new way of living is opened up to us. The better way to live begins to unfold before us! Following Jesus to the cross is the way to this life.

I want to be clear about the better way of living that Jesus wants to enfold in each one of our lives. Some of it will take time. It's not like we, ourselves, or our lives immediately become perfect the instant we choose Jesus. We need to unlearn our old ways and begin to learn the better ways. Time, in the hands of Jesus, is a

The Way of the Cross

powerful tool in ridding us of the old way of life and helping us step into the better way. Jesus is gracious. Jesus is patient. And Jesus is clear. He will help us live this new life out.

In working out how to follow the better way of Jesus, the following passage has been one of deep encouragement to me:

> *"Since you have been raised to new life with Christ, set your sights on the realities of heaven, where Christ sits in the place of honor at God's right hand. Think about the things of heaven, not the things of earth. For you died to this life, and your real life is hidden with Christ in God. And when Christ, who is your life, is revealed to the whole world, you will share in all his glory."* Colossians 3:1-4

When we choose to say "yes" to Jesus, the old way of living dies. A new life, a life hidden in Christ, takes its place. This hidden life in Him is far better than the old one we gave up. I like to think of us being hidden in Christ as when a man finds a treasure and chooses to hide it.[13] When Christ found us, He paid a high price through laying down His own life to obtain us. Yet, because of His joy in this new treasure, He did it gladly. Now possessing this treasure as His own, He does what anyone would! He takes us and hides us away in a special place.

Jesus will take good care of what He paid a high price for. He deeply values us. He will protect us. Jesus paid too much for our lives to be with Him to let someone else take us from Him. Now, with us being His treasure, He will fight to protect us. He is willing to go to battle for us. He will take care of us, defend us, and treasure us.

Can you imagine that? A life so valued by God that He considers us something worth hiding, valuing, and protecting. Yes, that God-action towards humanity is aimed directly at you and me. This hidden life is a good life! But in order to obtain it, we must die to our way of life that we get from this world. One life is given in exchange for another: the dead life for the hidden life. Let me assure you, this hidden life is far better.

If you look at the passage in Colossians 3, the next 11 verses go into a practical explanation of what this hidden way life ought to look like. The writer tells us about what brings death and needs to be rid from our lives. Things like greed, lust, and rage must be rooted out. The writer also tells us the new kinds of things that should take the place of those former things: kindness, forgiveness, gentleness, and love.

What does this context imply? The practical framework for living in this better way of life is built directly upon the Biblical understanding that we must die to the old life and step into the new life.[14] Christ alone allows us to die to the old life and be found in the better life, the hidden life, with Him. Only by following Jesus to the cross are we actually able to live out this better way.

That Biblical understanding is what much of this book has explored so far. We've looked at the death our current way of living brings as the fruit of humanity's own corrupted choices. We've considered the way God intended for us to live from the very beginning and how we are able to experience that better life once again. For much of the rest of this book, we will consider the practical means of experiencing this better way of living.

The Bible, which reveals the better way to us, is not just an ancient manuscript. It is God's direct words to us about how to live right now, in the present day. And it is always practical! His words, through the Bible, are an invitation into the better way in our everyday life. When the Bible speaks to any topic, it directs us towards the better way that leads to life. When the Bible speaks to addiction, it always points us to a better way. When the Bible speaks of family and sexuality, it points us to a better way. When the Bible speaks of relationships, success, or how we engage our world, it points us to a better way.

The practical isn't boring. The practical is where the better way of Jesus fleshed out in our life becomes even more wonderful. The practical details are where we get to see His ever-good intentions towards us more clearly demonstrated.

So let's look at the very tangible portions of the better way Jesus invites us into. Let's examine our paradigms of life, discard what is left behind from our old way, and step into the better way. May we remember that Jesus is kind to us in our weaknesses. Jesus wants to

The Better Way

help us when we turn to Him. Jesus wants us to experience His better way.

May we recognize the ways that lead to death and choose to live in His ways that lead to life!

Part 2: Living the Better Way

Chapter 7

The Way of Freedom

"So if the Son sets you free, you are truly free." John 8:36

There is a wild experience to be lived that comes from leaving one community and joining another. The summer between my freshman and sophomore years of high school, my family moved from the suburbs of Minneapolis to a small town in northwest Iowa. We moved from a metropolitan area of over 3 million people to a small town of 6,000. We left suburbia for a rural town hundreds of miles away, deep into the thick of farm country. As you would imagine, things were different in our new small town compared to where we had come from in the suburbs.

Shockingly, this transition went very well. We loved our small town of Estherville, Iowa. The people were kind. Our church contained many people that would become dear friends. I was able to quickly get a job at a grocery where I learned invaluable life skills. The movie theater tickets were only $5 each with an extra $1 discount for a matinee. And there were enough fast-food restaurants nearby to blow all of my newly earned money with my newfound friends. It was a good place to be as a teenager.

The Better Way

There were, however, some things that we had to learn when we freshly arrived from the big city. There were new cultural norms for us to embrace in this new town. The way people talked, related to one another, the clothes they wore, and even what they ate were different to us. For instance, cinnamon bread lathered in Cheese Whiz was considered a local delicacy. For two weeks each summer, hundreds of kids were shipped into the middle of corn fields for an activity called "detasseling" where they were paid more money than I could make in two months. Our high school's most important homecoming activity largely centered around toilet papering the school and running from the police. I also found that my 2010s taste in skinny jeans and band t-shirts made me stand out in a way I didn't exactly want. These norms weren't necessarily bad, but they were deeply ingrained into the culture of the town.

What's fascinating about cultural norms is that they are so pervasive and considered so "normal" that we often don't know they exist. They are the water in which we swim. Norms can be so widely accepted that countless people will look past a bizarre activity or practice because we assume everyone else in the world does it too. Most cultural norms are harmless and are really a matter of preference, like my hometown eating Cheese Whiz on cinnamon bread. Some cultural norms, however, are unhelpful or even outright wrong.

The Way of Freedom

Over the course of human history, there have been things that have been normalized in a culture that we would widely condemn today. In the pre-Civil War American South, slavery was normalized as an economic necessity. Yet today, we revile such an evil practice that dehumanizes people and have proven it to be an economically destructive force. Even the abhorrent practice of cannibalism has been culturally accepted in certain human societies. Things that we consider backwards today like women being unable to vote, child labor, or forced religious conversion were once widely accepted practices. Even though these ideas or activities are wrong, they were normal to the culture of the day.

This begs the question for us today: What might have we normalized in our current cultural moment that shouldn't be? What might be considered culturally normal, maybe even celebrated, that is actually a form of evil?

As someone whom I deeply respect proposed we have normalized "bondage".[15] Bondage is being held captive, enslaved, or oppressed by something or someone. It is the opposite of freedom. Bondage is being ruled by something. Bondage is being bound by something and unable to escape. Bondage is evil. It was never meant to be a part of our way of living. Yet, we have normalized the experience of living in bondage.

The Better Way

The kind of bondage I am referring to isn't a physical form. The kind of bondage I am addressing is one that is mental, emotional, and spiritual. It is found in countless living rooms, bedrooms, workplaces, and schools across our society. This kind of bondage can be just as real and actively damaging as physical bondage is. And it's permeated into the hearts of nearly every person in our world today.

Think about it. If bondage is being ruled or enslaved by something, then what rules our hearts? Have we let our hearts, our minds, and our emotions become enslaved by anything? Have we as a culture released control of our emotions, our thoughts, and our actions to someone or something else?

I would emphatically shout, "YES!" Our greatest bondage is to the activities of life that we think bring pleasure.

The proof of this is demonstrated in the way people choose to live. The rulers of people today are not human slave masters but activities and guilty pleasures. For instance, the average American spends over 74 days (4.9 hours per day)[16] a year watching TV. If the average person lives to 77, that means we will spend 15.6 of those years watching TV. Teenagers, between the ages of 13-19, spend an average of 4.8 hours per day[17] engaging on social media. That's an additional 15 years of life spent engaging a device. Don't let the blandness of statistics cause you to read past this truth. Re-read those numbers. This is

STAGGERING. What do you think rules the hearts and minds of people in our culture?

Entertainment and media usage alone could easily indict our world as living in bondage. That reference point doesn't include anything else that might rule our hearts that have become widely accepted in our culture. Consider these other forms of bondage: 70% of US men aged 18-34 have admitted to visiting a pornographic site in the past month.[18] Over 21% of US adults admit to binge drinking in the past month.[19] In young adults aged 19-30, 11% report using marijuana on a daily basis, and 43% report using it at least once in the last year.[20] Though our culture has celebrated these highly damaging activities, these aren't just a means of experiencing pleasure. Each one of these vices can and will rule over people. What started as something fun for many of us has turned into something we cannot escape from. These things, we are told, are good and our experience is normal. Yet, addiction is also very real. Life altering bondage is real.

Maybe you have found yourself in bondage to something. I know I have. In the place of bondage, we can't quit. We can't get out. The bondage rules our hearts, our emotions, and our thought life. We are so often stuck in our inability to break ourselves free from it that hopelessness takes its place right alongside the bondage we have conceded to. Our oppressors, in this case, are not other people. Our oppressors are bondages that we have gladly taken with the promise that they would bring us joy or pleasure. That was a lie. We were duped, and now we are stuck. In chains. In bondage. This is the way of living our world brings us into.

With the promise of pleasure, the way of our world leads us into bondage. In contrast, it is with the promise of power that the better way, found in Jesus, leads us into freedom. I say "the promise of power" because that is what is needed to break us out of bondage. Bondage is powerful. We are unable to overcome it on our own. Something stronger than the chains of our own bondage must come to set us free. That is exactly what Jesus declares He wants to do for us.

"The Spirit of the Lord is upon me, for he has anointed me to bring Good News to the poor. He has sent me to proclaim that captives will be released, that the blind will see, that the oppressed will be set free, and that the time of the Lord's favor has come." Luke 4:18-19

These are the words Jesus proclaimed right as He began announcing the better way for humanity. At the beginning of His moment in the spotlight, He announced Good News for you and me. Jesus announced a life changing experience for those of us found in bondage. FREEDOM. For all those who are oppressed. LIBERTY. For all those who are held captive. Jesus wants us to be bound to nothing in this world. His Good desire is that we would be people who are free. The better way that Jesus provides does not lead us into chains, but freedom.

Jesus then goes on to back up His words with actions. Remarkably powerful actions.

"God anointed Jesus of Nazareth with the Holy Spirit and with power. Then Jesus went around doing good and healing all who were oppressed by the devil, for God was with him." Acts 10:38

Jesus did what He said He would do. He went around healing all those who were oppressed! The devil, the deceiver from the garden, still wants to bind people. Jesus goes straight for the serpent's power, demolishes it, and then sets us free. Throughout the four books in the Bible called The Gospels, Jesus went on a rampage against anything that was putting people into bondage. Jesus set people free from disease, physical disabilities, demonic possession, greed[21], sexual immorality[22], and much more. In fact, Jesus went about doing so much good, setting so many people free, that the Bible says it would fill up every book in existence if we tried to record it.[23]

Jesus has continued to set millions of people free since His arrival on Earth two millennia ago. I would know because I am one of them. Bondage took ahold of my life as a teenager in the form of pornography. At first, the experience would bring me momentary pleasure. It would satisfy the corrupted human nature that exists within me. Then, it would leave me feeling empty and hollow. For years, I was eaten up on the inside by this bondage that I knew was holding me back. I even tried to stop by myself. It didn't work. Going head-to-head with bondage, we humans will always lose. I was defeated. I couldn't say "no" to my bondage even if I tried. Bondage had become my ruler.

Then, around my senior year of high school, I had a life changing conversation with my father. He, obviously, was saddened by the bondage in my life. Yet, he graciously reminded me of the freedom that Jesus offers. He urged me to bring it to Jesus. So somewhat awkwardly with my own dad, I brought my bondage of pornography to Jesus. I felt the love of Jesus so strongly in my weakness. His forgiveness became so real in that moment. Then, Jesus unleashed His power in my life. He began to set me free. It wasn't instantaneous, but I had finally discovered the power to say "no." After a few years of saying "no" to this bondage alongside other men, who themselves had been set free, I stepped into freedom. The bondage of pornography has no place in my life any longer. It has no power in my life. Jesus set me free.

"Jesus replied, 'I tell you the truth, everyone who sins is a slave of sin. A slave is not a permanent member of the family, but a son is part of the family forever. So if the Son sets you free, you are truly free.'" John 8:34-36

The Way of Freedom

At some level, each one of us is in some sort of bondage. Bondage is normal in our world. Our old, tired way of living will always lead us to bondage. But in the Better Way of Jesus, bondage isn't normal, freedom is. Through Jesus, bondage loses its power. Jesus Himself brings to bear His power in our life to give us freedom. And when Jesus sets us free, we are truly free. This is the better way.

If you are reading this book today and you know you are in bondage, there is Good News for you. Bondage does not have to be your ruler. You don't have to live a life oppressed and incapable of escaping from under its power. Jesus wants to and can set you free. It's very possible. It's very real. Don't live another day under its power. Instead, invite Jesus into your life to show you how to live in freedom. Invite His power to come and set you free. Let Him tear off your chains of bondage and bring you into the life of freedom you can only find through Him. This is the better way of living in Jesus.

Living the Better Way:

Now that we know Jesus's better way, what do we do with it? Consider the questions below. Let Jesus lead you into what life in His better way looks like. An example prayer is written below for what turning to Jesus for help can look like in living this better way.

1. What might I be in bondage to in my own life that I have normalized? Is there something that I cannot stop or is controlling my life/actions in an unhealthy way?

2. How would my life look different if I was set free from that bondage? How would I act, talk, and think differently?

Turning to Jesus: Jesus, you see me in my bondage. Jesus, you know I am unable to break free from some of these things that control me. Come, set me free! Thank you for your power that breaks the power of bondage and sets my life into freedom. Thank you for the better way that exists in freedom. Help me to live according to your way.

Chapter 8

The Way of Fullness

"...I have come that they may have life, and have it to the full."
John 10:10 (NIV)

My parents have always been runners, and I took up the hobby in college. It proved to be remarkably helpful in relieving stress, burning off extra energy after hours of studying calculus, and processing through my emotions. All vital things for a college student in that season of life. Even though I was not a collegiate level athlete, I became very disciplined in my years at college. Running was something that I did six days a week, and this rhythm continued well after I graduated as well. As a runner and eager for a challenge, I loved to run distances that pushed myself. Then, in the fall after my senior year of college, I decided to embark on the endeavor of running a marathon.

My training plan was basic and something I created myself. My approach was not innovative. It simply involved working hard enough so that 26 miles of continuous running would be somewhat doable. Four days per week involved 30 minutes of intense cardio or a fast-paced run. Another day of the week I would run 8-10 miles at a more measured pace. My last day of training before my rest day would always consist of a long

The Better Way

run. At first the distance started out at 10 miles. Then 12. Then 14. Then 16. Then 18. It was on my 18-mile run that things went sideways for me.

Since I hate working out on a full stomach, I only had two packets of oatmeal and a cup of coffee before my 18-mile run. It was a light 320 calories to start out a 2.5-hour long run. The first 15 miles went by just like my other long runs had. Steady, strong, and consistent. At around mile 16, I began to smell the McDonalds near my parents' house. Oh, I was hungry! My stomach started to churn and my mouth watered at the smell of their french fries. Around mile 17, I had to stop for a traffic light. My legs were starting to feel really weak, and it was difficult to get moving again. Within a half mile of my parents' home, about 17.5 miles into the run, I hit it. For the first time in my life, I hit the fabled "runner's wall."

My balance began to falter. My legs started to feel like jelly. My body was thrown into chaos. I actually do not know if I could have finished that last ½ mile, even if I pushed with everything that was left within me. In shame, I had to finish the last half mile not running but hobbling slowly home. What happened? With all of my consistent training, how could I end a run this way?

The "runner's wall" means you physically run out of energy. My muscles, which are filled with glycogen as a quick energy source, completely ran out of readily available energy.[24] Plus, I didn't eat anything for the entirety of the run, so my body had nothing new to be nourished by. I was running as hard as I could for 2.5 hours and didn't once think about how I was going to meet my body's energy needs. Because I did not fill my body with what I needed, I began to physically fail. I had run too long on empty.

This experience has long made me wonder that if this can happen in our physical bodies after running on empty for too long, who is to say that something similar cannot happen in our mental and emotional being? Who is to say that something like that can't happen at the soul-level? What happens if we run too long with our souls on empty? Human beings obviously have physical bodies with physical needs that have to be met. All things considered, we are mostly able to do that. But what happens if we don't meet the needs of our own souls?

We don't need to look far to see that hypothetical actually manifested in our world. Unfortunately, the masses of people in our materially privileged, Western society often walking around with deep emotional deficits and unmet soul-level needs demonstrate this harsh reality. As mentioned earlier, we are the most emotionally unhealthy we have ever been. Since 1930, there has been a clear trend of young adults in the United States experiencing depression more and more.[25] An even more tragic manifestation of this unhealth is growing too. Suicide is the 10th leading cause of death of adults in the United States.[26] Each year it is estimated that over 380,000 adults made emergency room visits for self-inflicted injuries, and more than 10 million adults have reported having suicidal thoughts in the past year.[27]

If the way of living in our current world has resulted in such a wretched state of the human soul, something has gone horribly, horribly wrong. This is never the way we were intended to live. It was this way of living, filled with suffering and death, that God wanted to prevent us from experiencing. Yet, here we are. Depressed. Anxious. Lonely. Riddled with thoughts about life not having value. We are an empty people.

Thankfully, God has not chosen to leave us in our sorry state. In His Good nature, He has provided a way out for us. He has given us a way for the deep needs of our soul to be met. In His wonderful plan for redeeming humanity back from our own corrupted way, He offers a redeeming work for our souls. Jesus, who knows the effects of decay on our souls from living in our own way, and who is the very way to life Himself, says this:

> *"The thief comes only to steal and kill and destroy; I have come that they may have life, and have it to the full."* John 10:10 (NIV)

Isn't that good news? Jesus desires that we may have life and life to the full. Abundant life. Not an empty life of depression. Not a life of anxiety. Not a life of weariness. Instead, He intends for us to live a life of abundance. Abundant joy. Abundant peace. Abundant rest. This is the way of life that Jesus longs to bring us into. He intends for us to experience life!

Jesus wants to meet the needs of our souls. So He does what He has done in every other situation for us. He gives us more of Himself. Jesus, the person Himself, is our great solution. He is our way to fullness.

"You will show me the way of life, granting me the joy of your presence and the pleasures of living with you forever." Psalm 16:11

JOY. Have you ever been around someone who is overflowing with joy? It's almost contagious. Have you ever been with someone who it was a pleasure to be with? We look forward to when we can be with them again. That is who Jesus is but to the infinite degree! And in the way of Jesus, He gives us Himself. He makes Himself accessible to us.

By giving us access to Himself, we get joy. There is a deep, soul-level joy experienced by being around the person who created and defined it. It is a joyful and pleasurable thing to know and be with God. This kind of joy supersedes all other emotions because it's not dependent on our circumstances. This joy goes about setting people free from the weight of hopelessness. This joy can be experienced in every moment of life because we are invited to be with God in every moment of life. Though sometimes we might choose lesser, His invitation into joy with Him will always remain. Today and every day, from here to eternity, He invites us to experience the joy and pleasure of being with Him!

I have never experienced more joy than when I have experienced closeness with God. Encountering His joy through His love has been life changing for me. Experiencing the joy of knowing that even my troubles in this life can be worked out for good by God has rooted out the hopelessness that can come with the human experience. I've also seen His joy at work in the lives of many people. In my own friends, I've seen them released from depression through the joy they found in Jesus.

Incredibly, I was able to watch as one of my closest friends, Riley, was released from the weight of depression by Jesus and began to experience real joy in his life. Here are his words:

"For years I was trapped in a place of depression. Life felt like it was pointless, and I was unable to experience any hope or excitement. Realizing that I couldn't save myself from my own sin, I felt trapped in hopelessness. Secret sin and the need to pretend like I was perfect was destroying my life. It wasn't until when I was in college and I came to the realization that Jesus died because He wanted me to be free, that I started to experience life. Trusting that God's way is better, I chose to let Jesus change my priorities and the way I was living. Jesus started to refine those secret sins and cynical ways of thinking out of my life. I replaced those sinful things with God's ways of living and a very real relationship with Jesus. It was only then, I was able to experience the joy and life that Jesus had come to give me. Hopelessness broke off my life. In having fresh hope in my heart, I began to be able to care about life again. It was as if Jesus replaced what was dull with living color."

Riley's experience with freedom from depression and into joy is what Jesus wants to do in the hearts of all people. Including you. We were never meant to stay stuck in hopelessness. We were never meant to be weighed down by depression. Instead of being stuck with the heaviness of despair, Jesus replaces it with the kind of joy that only comes from Him. As Riley said, Jesus wants to replace the dull and gloomy life with living color.

"I am leaving you with a gift—peace of mind and heart. And the peace I give is a gift the world cannot give. So don't be troubled or afraid." John 14:27

PEACE. What a wonderful word. What a wonderful thing for our souls to encounter. What a rare thing to find in our world. Yet, in spite of its rarity in our world today, Jesus offers it freely to us! There are no tricks. There are no games. He gives us the gift Himself. More still, His peace is better than the kind of peace this world offers. The kind of peace this world offers is often based on agreements between two parties known as "peace agreements." The kind of peace this world offers is based on circumstances, like being by a peaceful lake on a warm, sunny day. It's emotional, like one being at peace through the absence of emotional turmoil.

The kind of peace Jesus offers is far better. His peace is not an agreement, it's a gift. We get to accept it freely. His peace is not emotional, it's settled. On the cross, Jesus paid a high price for us to experience peace with God and peace in our hearts. That work has now been finished and it will not need to be done again. His peace is not circumstantial, it's the basis for courage in a world on fire. He promises a peace that is so resilient to worldly conditions that it is comparable to eating a feast in the presence of our enemies.[28]

The peace that Jesus provides is something that I got to experience acutely in 2020 when the world ground to a halt due to the Covid-19 Pandemic. In February, before the world shut down, I had become very anxious about Covid. I had seen it coming and knew that it was inevitable. This anxiety was unlike anything I had ever experienced before. I couldn't sleep. It dominated my thoughts. There was a tightness in my chest for over a week. After realizing that I was incapable of changing the circumstances of our world, I finally decided to turn to Jesus.

That's when the entire year for me turned a corner. In the early days of March 2020, when the world was shutting down, the peace of Jesus met me in my stress and worry. It filled my life in a new way. Instead of being worried, I felt settled. Instead of being shaken daily by the new Covid-19 statistics, I had encountered a hope that was unshakeable. Courage, which is a direct by-product of Jesus's peace, filled my heart. By God's grace, 2020 was a wonderful year for me and my family. We had experienced a supernatural peace in the way of Jesus.

Jesus offers this kind of peace to all. His peace. Jesus offers His peace to you, today. We were never meant to live in a constant state of worry and anxiety. Yet, that is what is constantly produced from our own way of living. The only way to experience real and unchanging peace is in the way of Jesus. He is the better way.

"Then Jesus said, "Come to me, all of you who are weary and carry heavy burdens, and I will give you rest. Take my yoke upon you. Let me teach you, because I am humble and gentle at heart, and you will find rest for your souls. For my yoke is easy to bear, and the burden I give you is light." Matthew 11:28-30

The Better Way

REST. This might be one of the most elusive things in our world. I'm not talking about sleep, which is hard to come by for me in our current season of having young children in our home. I mean a rest that comes from knowing that the work needed to prove our own worth is finished. This rest doesn't come from the avoidance of work, it comes from the fact that the work is already done.

We have all experienced the absence of rest in our souls. It brings turmoil. It brings stress. It brings the need to hustle. Hurry is a common symptom. Some of us drive our minds and our bodies into the ground trying to work hard to prove ourselves. Burnout begins to slowly kill us. Others of us know that we can never work hard enough to prove ourselves, so we get lazy and slothful. Then, shame smacks us in the face when we get up every morning because we know we have neglected the hard work. This incessant need to work and prove ourselves is another by-product of our corrupt way of living.

Work is not a curse. Work was, in the Garden of Eden, incorporated in the way God intended for us to live. The curse is the unending, fruitless work that attempts to earn back what we lost in the Garden. When we left the garden as a result of sin, we were cut off from God and put under the curse of death. Ever since then, the human experience has involved attempting to work ourselves back to God and find a way to life. This is not the way we were intended to live.

Jesus is the way back to God. Jesus is the way to life. Both of the things that we work incessantly for, Jesus chooses to give us for free. Jesus can give it to us because He has done all the work for us on the cross. The sacrificial work that He performed on the cross on our behalf gives a chance to return back to God. The work of the cross is what lifts the curse of death. Now, there is no work left for us to do! In the way that Jesus provides, all we have to do is step into His rest.

This rest removes the need to prove ourselves through our accomplishments. We don't need to fall into workaholism and sacrifice ourselves for Earthly achievements to prove our worth or value anymore. Jesus has already proven our value in how He gave up His life for us on the cross. This rest removes the need to work our way back to God through religious adherence or following a list of rules. Though we follow Jesus's commands as a demonstration of love and acknowledgement that His ways are better, following rules alone does not get us back to God. It is Jesus's blood shed that does. This rest releases us to live life without the fear of death. Though physical death will come, the death of our soul and spirit are transformed into eternal life. It is through Jesus's death on the cross that we get to experience life.

Our world is running on empty. Our corrupted way of living has failed to meet the needs of our soul. We were never

The Better Way

meant to live empty lives. We were never meant to have our experience in life be as hollow as it has become. Jesus longs to meet the needs of our souls. He wants to fill us with life. Life abundantly. Life to the full. Let us press into His way that leads to life.

Living the Better Way:

Consider the questions below. Let Jesus lead you into what life in His better way looks like.

1. How have I been running on empty? Is there something in my life that leads me to feeling empty? What emotional/soul-level need do I have that I should ask Jesus to help fill?

2. How would my life look different if I let Jesus meet my soul-level need? How would I act, talk, and think differently if Jesus gave me His joy, rest, and peace?

Turning to Jesus: Jesus, you know my emptiness. Jesus, you know I am unable to fill the deep needs of my soul. Come, fill my life! Thank you for your generous love in giving me your joy, your peace, and your rest. Thank you for the better way that comes from my soul being filled by you. Help me to live according to your ways.

Chapter 9

The Way of Relationship

"Together as one body, Christ reconciled both groups to God by means of his death on the cross, and our hostility toward each other was put to death."
Ephesians 2:16

The end of my junior year of college was a wild one. At 8 AM on that Thursday of finals week, I completed my two-hour long Analytical Chemistry exam in 45 minutes and sprinted out of the classroom. Riding my longboard as fast as I could, I arrived at my car. Within minutes I had left town and begun a 10-hour drive to the edge of civilization. My destination was a boat ramp on the Missouri River in Washburn, North Dakota.

My cousin, who I had been best friends with for my entire life, was getting married later that weekend. His bachelor party was that Thursday. I couldn't miss it! The plan was to canoe a few miles down the river, spend the night on an island on the river, and canoe the remaining distance downriver to the outskirts of Bismarck. The caveat was that the party was embarking on the voyage around 2 PM, and my ETA to Washburn was 7 PM. The party was going to leave a lone kayak for me to take down the river, in the hopes that I would catch up to them before nightfall. It was a solid plan in my mind.

The Better Way

Apparently, the plan didn't sit as well with my parents, my cousin's parents, or the parents of my cousin's new bride.

The entire 10-hour car ride consisted of sporadic phone calls from my mom, my dad, my aunt, my uncle, and my cousins. All of the parents were telling me that I was risking death. They thought that the river was too cold and too dangerous for me to kayak down by myself that close to sunset. My cousins, meanwhile, believed that it was totally doable. Plus, they really didn't want me to miss out on the party. With the assurance of my cousins, I decided to disregard the concerns of our parents and head down the river by myself. I put the kayak into the river around 7:15 PM and began the 5ish-mile trek down river.

The river was huge and freezing cold. There were countless obstacles and many turns. The current was faster in some spots and stagnant in others. On top of all of this, I was awful at kayaking, so I was constantly getting wet from the splashes of my own paddle. With each passing minute, the sky was getting darker as sunset was getting closer. With less and less visibility, I began to use what can only be described as God's divine providence in my life. My cellphone had a working cell signal. Every 15 minutes or so, I would call one of my cousins down river. They had been down the river only hours earlier, so they were able to encourage me and give directions through the many obstacles found along the way.

The Way of Relationship

Finally, at 9 PM I spotted the fire they had started for me on the shore of the island. With great excitement, I paddled so hard that I soaked myself to the bone. At one point, I hit a sandbar big enough that I was forced to get out of the kayak and drag the small boat nearly 100 ft to cross it. Eventually, I arrived at shore. What happened next was an almost heavenly experience.

Right when I got to shore, 10 of my closest family and friends welcomed me with shouts and whoops. They pulled my kayak to shore. Each gave me a big hug. As they ushered me to the camp further inland, one of my cousins handed me a cold can of Coca-Cola. Another cousin gave me a freshly cooked burger. Warming myself by the fire, filling my hungry stomach with food, and surrounded by some of the dearest people in my life after I had just endured one of the most daring experiences of my life was unreal. It was heaven-like. Rarely have I felt so supported, encouraged, admired, and appreciated as I told them about my solo journey down the river. The party wasn't even planned for me, but it was a mountain top moment. These people, with whom I have such deep connection, received me so well. I remember thinking, "I wish I always felt like this."

What I experienced on that island in the middle of the Missouri River on that brisk North Dakota night was deep relationship. It was a rich experience with community. That moment felt so blissful and so wonderful because it was a taste of the way of living we are intended for. Humans, all of us, are designed for deep, genuine connection with one another. We are hard-wired for relationship. This is one of the reasons Genesis 2 says, *"It is not good for man to be alone."* We were never meant to be alone. We were never meant to live life in isolation. Even while being in perfect relationship with God, He still decided to give us each other.

Unfortunately, our lived experiences are often so different from that ideal. Isolation is how many of us are experiencing life more and more. Think of the stereotypical American suburban lifestyle that reinforces our isolation. Each morning, we get into our cars parked in our garages, without having to talk to our neighbors or passersby, to drive to work. We go to an office or workplace where we shut the door or put in headphones to avoid conversation in an effort to be more productive. In the elevator or standing in line, we don't look up from our phones as we scroll through social media and check the news. We then drive home, open our garage doors, and head inside. DoorDash will leave the food at our doorstep for supper so we don't even have to greet the delivery driver. We come up with a wide range of excuses to give to our friends in an effort to stay at home so we can watch the next four episodes of the Netflix show we are bingeing. Then, we go to bed without saying "hi" to any of our family members, only to spend the next hour watching TikTok by ourselves in our dark bedrooms.

Now, I know those might be over-generalizations, but how many of us have done some of those things? Those particularly Western tendencies of self-isolation don't even include the wide variety of other, normal factors that drive us away from each other. Things like political tensions, ethnic divides, family feuds, romantic drama, or conflicts with friends. We, as people, have a terrible tendency of driving ourselves apart into our own isolated little silos. In those silos, we get through our lonely life by self-medicating with technology and entertainment. Meanwhile, our deficit of genuine relational connection grows.

Here is the hard reality we all must grapple with: loneliness is a scourge in our human experience, and it only seems to be increasing in recent years. In a survey about friendships among Americans from 1990 compared to 2021, empirical data demonstrates that we are less connected than we were decades ago.[29] The number of Americans who said they do not have any close friendships increased from 3% to 12%. More shockingly, only 13% of Americans in 2021 said they had 10 or more close friends compared to a whopping 33% that had 10 or more close friends in 1990! We apparently had a lot more friends three decades ago than we do now! With 53% of college students[30] and over 33% of older adults[31] (>45 years old) reporting being lonely, we are all feeling more disconnected from others.

The Better Way

Unsurprisingly, loneliness and social isolation are detrimental to our health. According to the US Surgeon General, loneliness "is associated with a greater risk of cardiovascular disease, dementia, stroke, depression, anxiety, and premature death. The mortality impact of being socially disconnected is similar to that caused by smoking up to 15 cigarettes a day."[32] Yikes. To say that we were designed to experience connection with others is an understatement. It's absolutely vital for any sort of quality of life. Yet, once again, our current way of living drives us further away from genuine relationships than to them. There has to be a better way of living than this.

Community, relationships, and friendship are deeply embedded aspects in the way of Jesus. While we often understand that Jesus makes a way for us to experience a restored connection with God, we often don't recognize that Jesus also makes a way to experience a restored connection with each other. Jesus doesn't want people to be angry at each other. Jesus doesn't want us to be divided and bitter. Nor does He want people to experience connection that consists only of a pleasant smile and a wave. Our relationships with each other are meant to be something much more meaningful than that. So how does Jesus do this? How does He accomplish this work of restoring us to deep relationships with each other?

That work is accomplished by way of Christ on the cross:

The Way of Relationship

"For Christ himself has brought peace to us. He united Jews and Gentiles into one people when, in his own body on the cross, he broke down the wall of hostility that separated us. He did this by ending the system of law with its commandments and regulations. He made peace between Jews and Gentiles by creating in himself one new people from the two groups. Together as one body, Christ reconciled both groups to God by means of his death on the cross, and our hostility toward each other was put to death." Ephesians 2:14-16

With the infinite number of ways that we can divide ourselves from one another, Jesus does something remarkable. Jesus, through the cross, makes a way for all human individuals to be a part of a newly unified people. These people are no longer separated by their ethnic or racial distinctions. These people are no longer separated by religious upbringings or socioeconomic statuses. Instead, their connection with each other comes from choosing the way of Jesus. In the way Jesus provides for us, He ends the hostility between peoples and unites us in Him.

These newly unified people in Jesus are called the Church. Though there are many different local expressions, the Church consists of anyone who has chosen to follow in the way of Jesus. In this new people, the Church, Jesus gives us a new way of relating to one another.

"So now I am giving you a new commandment: Love each other. Just as I have loved you, you should love each other. Your love for one

The Better Way

another will prove to the world that you are my disciples." John 13:34-35

The way of treating one another, commanded by Jesus Himself, is to love each other. He asks us to love each other as He has loved us. And how did Jesus love us? He laid down His life for us! Jesus asks His new people to love each other so much so as to be willing to die for one another. Dang, that's a high bar. Not only will this be the standard of His Church, but it will be so abundantly obvious that this kind of love exists between His people that the whole world will know about it. Jesus's command to love is so strong that He warns us if we do not forgive each other that we risk not receiving our own forgiveness from God.[33] Again, Jesus's standard for love among His people is high.

Jesus also details many more ways He expects us to act towards one another. We are told that Jesus's people should bear each other's burdens[34] and make allowance for each other's faults.[35] The Bible goes on to say that we should regard others as better than ourselves[36] and outdo each other in showing honor.[37] Let me point out the obvious, those relationship qualities sound other-worldly. They are. The way of living our world offers can never produce these kinds of relationships. Instead, the relationships in our world commonly produce anger, strife, and division. Jesus's directives for us are very different. This is the better way.

The Way of Relationship

If those traits are to be exemplified in Jesus's people, then His people must spend enough time around each other to have a chance to practice this out. We can't make room for each other's faults if we aren't around someone long enough to see their faults. It's impossible to outdo each other in honor without giving the space in our lives it takes to honor each other. If we are to forgive each other, we must be with each other enough to have been wronged by another. In order to experience this kind depth of community, we have to participate in life with each other. There's no other way to do it.

This is why the better way of Jesus calls us to be a part of His Church. We need to find a local expression of Jesus's people by joining a church in our community. A church is a gathering of people who have chosen the way of Jesus and want to be unified together in Him. In that gathering of people, people who are eager to experience the kind of community described in the Bible live life close enough with each other to practice it out. If we aren't a part of a church community, we won't get that kind of experience. If we are absent, we will never have a chance of being in those kinds of relationships.

My own personal life has been deeply impacted by the people Jesus chooses to unify together in His Church. My parents, who were pastors since before I could even form memories, have always brought me into church communities. In those communities, I have seen both good and bad. I have seen

The Better Way

people hurt each other. I have seen people gossip about others. I have seen my own parents get treated awfully and screamed at by people in church. Yet, this has not tainted my view of this heaven-inspired community. People are people. They are messy and full of their own issues. The reality of people being sinful and treating each other poorly does not invalidate the need for this Jesus-centered community in our lives.

The friendships I have through my own church experience are the deepest I have ever formed. My roommates through college, who fought alongside me and encouraged me in my deepest moments of addiction and rejection, are friends I have gained through being a part of a church. Some of the most significant voices of encouragement and mentorship in my life are people I got to know through being a part of a church. Even my cousins, who I journeyed down the Missouri River with, are people who have chosen the way of Jesus. We have hurt and offended each other. Yet, we are united through Jesus, so we choose to forgive each other. They have honored me dozens of times over by laying down their own preferences and priorities for my benefit.

Yes, I have had moments where I have gotten hurt. Then, I got the chance to love like Jesus does and forgive. Yes, I have at times been at odds with important decisions people, even dear friends, have made in the Church. Then, I have gotten a chance to regard others as better than myself and outdo them

The Way of Relationship

with honor. I have even felt the feeling of being lonely in moments throughout my life. But have I ever been truly alone without someone to turn to for help in the Church? NEVER. There is no other group of people on the planet where you can experience such deep relationship. Even if we have little in common with others in a Jesus-centered community, Jesus unites us. Jesus invites us into being in deep relationship with His people. It is a critical part of the better way of living Jesus invites us into.

The Bible gives us a critical directive regarding our participation in this community of people united through Jesus. We are to not stop meeting together and stirring each other up to love and good works.[38] Even if the world ends. Even if another pandemic hits. Even if we are hurt by others in the Church. We must continue being with the people Jesus wants to unite together in His Church. If we fail to participate in this way, we will fail to experience the fullness of relationship provided for us in the way of Jesus. It's really the better way.

Living the Better Way:

Consider the questions below. Let Jesus lead you into what life in His better way looks like.

1. Have I chosen to not participate in Jesus's Church in any way? What past misconceptions or even past hurts might I have that have been an obstacle for me?

2. How would my life look different if I participated in the relationships Jesus wants to give me access to in His Church? How different would my decisions and time investments be?

Turning to Jesus: Jesus, you know my need for relationships. Jesus, you know how I might have neglected your better way of participating with your people. Reframe my misconceptions about your Church. Help me forgive those in the Church that may have hurt me. Thank you for your generous provision in giving me a people to belong to. Thank you for the better way that comes from being in relationships with your people. Help me to live according to your ways.

Chapter 10

The Way of Intimacy

"This explains why a man leaves his father and mother and is joined to his wife, and the two are united into one." Genesis 2:24

The day of my and my wife's wedding was a hot and muggy June day. We had wisely chosen to have our ceremony and reception inside air-conditioned buildings. As we left the ceremony with our wedding party to go take pictures at a nearby park, clouds began to build in the sky above us. After far too long in the heat and mosquito-infested woods, we headed towards the location of our reception. While we were taking a few more pictures at a quant pond outside of our reception venue, it began to rain. If the tradition of rain on your wedding day is a sign of good luck, we were about to become the luckiest couple alive!

During the reception, which was filled with amazing food and one of the best dance parties I've ever attended, the heavens opened up. Rain began to come down so hard that the view out of the prominent wall of windows located behind the head table was completely obscured. While we were sharing speeches and filling our stomachs with fantastic cupcakes, the rain poured down relentlessly. About the time we decided to depart from our reception, there was a small break in the rain.

The Better Way

We took our window and left the reception venue to the cheers of our closest friends and family. It was an exhilarating moment.

We had decided ahead of time that we weren't going to change out of our wedding outfits until we arrived at our hotel for that night. In our full wedding attire, we drove ahead into one of the biggest rainstorms Iowa had seen in years. Some places recorded nine inches that night alone. The rain began to pour down once again as we drove the 45 minutes to our hotel. The water was beginning to run out of places to go. At one terrifying moment, the road we were driving on was submerged in water. The other side of the freeway had completely stopped, but the water wasn't quite deep enough on our side to stop traffic. As the excitement of a hotel room to ourselves on our wedding night lay ahead, I was committed to drive through any depth of water to reach our destination. Miraculously, we made it! After I dropped Katie off at the front door, I raced through the parking lot. I was soaked in the pouring rain. Though sopping wet, we were ecstatic to have safely reached our wedding night hotel room.

That wedding night contained our first moments together as a married couple. We were just stepping into an entirely new life together. In the days and months later, we began to experience the kind of intimacy and closeness that marriage should bring. Our marriage brought a relational closeness with each other unlike anything we had ever experienced before. For us, marriage also opened up the world of physical intimacy that has become such a unifying part of our relationship. In marriage, we were stepping into depths of intimacy that are not experienced in any other human relationship. God, in the perfect way of living that He designed for us, gave marriage to us as the pinnacle of relational and physical intimacy. Marriage is a gift of intimate relationship for humanity.

The gift of marriage goes all the way back to the beginning. Before humanity chose its own corrupt way, and while we were still living in the way of perfection with God, God built marriage for us. Marriage was sown into creation itself. Consider God's words about man when He first created Adam:

"Then the Lord God said, 'It is not good for the man to be alone. I will make a helper who is just right for him.'" Genesis 2:18

God knew that he was giving the man unlimited access to Himself in the Garden of Eden. Yet, the man was still in need of another kind of relationship. So what did God do? God looked at all the animals and found none worthy of being a companion for man. He decided that He needed to do a new work. This new work would be the final piece of God's creation before He rested.

"Then the Lord God made a woman from the rib, and he brought her to the man. 'At last!' the man exclaimed. 'This one is bone from my

> *bone, and flesh from my flesh! She will be called 'woman,' because she was taken from 'man'.'"* Genesis 2:22-23

God made woman as a perfect helper for man. Now, this word helper doesn't mean "a person who washes my laundry" nor does it mean "a person who listens to my every command." This Hebrew word for helper, "ezer", has far more gravity than that. Every time "ezer" is used in the Old Testament, it is referring to God who helps or a military form of help.[39] The woman was created to be of such importance in helping man that she is most analogous to God helping man or military aid helping man.

Here's the takeaway: Men need women. Women need men. We are perfect complements to each other.

By creating us as perfect complements to each other, God created the beautiful, covenantal relationship of marriage. In the final sentences of the Bible's creation narrative, God introduces marriage to humanity:

> *"This explains why a man leaves his father and mother and is joined to his wife, and the two are united into one."* Genesis 2:24

WOW. Marriage is so critical to God's design that He pauses the creation account to define this foundational relationship. Later, during Jesus's time on the Earth, He doubles down on this way of living for living for humanity. In Matthew 19, Jesus repeated these exact words about men and women being united into one. But, He also does more. With the notable exception of infidelity, Jesus strongly condemns the tearing apart of a marriage. This is not what Jesus's disciples were expecting to hear in their divorce-riddled society.

> *"Since they are no longer two but one, let no one split apart what God has joined together."... Jesus replied, "Moses permitted divorce only as a concession to your hard hearts, but it was not what God had originally intended. And I tell you this, whoever divorces his wife and marries someone else commits adultery—unless his wife has been unfaithful."* Matthew 19:6,8-9

Marriage is a divine institution of deep intimacy. God crafted it uniquely to bless humanity. It's a spiritual union between a man and woman that is so wonderful that Jesus rebukes any attempt to cheapen it. Jesus explicitly affirms the creation narrative that marriage only exists between one man and one woman. He strongly rebukes adultery, divorce, and even lustful thoughts towards those we are not married to. This high respect for marriage was so unbelievable to Jesus's disciples that they wonder if "it's better not to get married."[40] Jesus, out of any human relationships, placed the highest value on marriage.

Does this mean everyone has to get married? No. Jesus clearly blesses those who remain unmarried for the sake of dedicating their lives more wholly to God.[41]

What this does mean is that God invited humanity to experience unparalleled intimacy inside of a lifelong committed marriage. This unrivaled intimacy is meant solely for a man and a woman bound together in marriage. Marriage is established through men and women committing themselves wholeheartedly and exclusively to each other. That commitment is so unifying that they are considered "one flesh". This oneness means two individuals say "goodbye" to their singleness and say "yes" to a lifelong union with another. In this place of oneness, we are meant to experience love unlike any other human relationship can offer. In this union, we are meant to give ourselves sacrificially for the benefit of our spouse. In marriage, complete vulnerability and precious intimacy are purposed to bind two together into one.

It is through this experience of being "one" in marriage that God gives sex as a gift of physical intimacy to man and woman.

"Now the man and his wife were both naked, but they felt no shame" Genesis 2:25

Sex, which is the physical representation of the greater spiritual union in marriage, was given to humanity without shame. Isn't that amazing? There was never meant to be any awkwardness in it. Sex was never intended to be anything to be embarrassed of. In marriage, sex can be experienced with full trust and complete openness to another who has pledged their life to you. In marriage, sex transforms from an act of self-pleasure into an act of bringing pleasure to your spouse. It is through the way of marriage that God intended for us to enjoy sex and bind us together in intimacy.

I realize that God's design for marriage and sex is actually considered quite counter-cultural. The average American now has more than 10 sex partners in their lifetime.[42] Marriage rates in the United States have declined to half of what they were in 1970.[43] Marriage is often thought of as an outdated concept. But in its decline, what have we profited? Are we and our society now better off without sex being saved for the sacredness of the marriage bed?

More still, sex outside of marriage between a man and woman has proven to be perilous. The rate of infidelity among married couples is less than half of that of those who are unmarried.[44] Without the lifelong union of two people, trust can more easily be broken. Without the confidence of being unified with the other person we are physically intimate with, shame and emotional pain are often the outcomes. Even the risk of physical disease is far more common in sex outside of marriage.[45] How can we give ourselves over fully to someone who we have no marriage bond with and not expect bad outcomes when it ends? Trust is far more easily broken without the commitment of marriage to hem in the physical risk that comes with having sex with someone. Tragically, we have adopted that painful experience as the "norm" in our culture. Think of the countless love songs and books that have been written about these kinds of heartbreaking experiences.

Yet, in contrast to that cultural norm, marriage stands as a healthier and far more secure way to experience the gift of sex. Sex inside of marriage is an objective good. Sex in marriage binds the two deeper into one. Sex in marriage is the ideal for physical intimacy. Social science backs this up. Married couples who attend church regularly report having better and more satisfied sex lives.[46] The fewer sexual partners an individual has throughout their life correlates to high levels of sexual satisfaction.[47] God has established marriage as the better way to experience physical and emotional intimacy.

For those who have already experienced physical intimacy outside of marriage, please know that this is not a message of condemnation. Instead, this is an invitation to a better way of living today. Jesus loves us so much that He not only died for us, but He also calls us out of the ways that He knows will bring pain into our lives. That includes the lesser forms of intimacy our world goads us into. Better yet, Jesus can purify our hearts. He can reorder any desires that are not in alignment with His. He can heal our wounded souls. He can recover what we think is permanently lost in this part of our life. Jesus lovingly stands ready today. He is inviting you and me into His way for us to enjoy this kind intimacy in our lives.

Even in the face of changing cultural norms, God's way of marriage continually proves its profoundly unique ability to provide us with intimacy. Let's choose what's better in God's intended way of living. May we aim to settle for nothing less than His better way of experiencing intimacy in our lives.

Living the Better Way:

Consider the questions below. Let Jesus lead you into what life in His better way looks like.

1. How have I misunderstood God's intentions for marriage and sex? How might I have fallen short of Jesus's way for intimacy?

2. How would my life look different if I were to follow Jesus's better way for intimacy? What hard conversations might I need to have or tough decisions might I have to make to follow Jesus's better way?

Turning to Jesus: Jesus, you know my past mistakes. Jesus, you know I am unable to live out your better way for intimacy without your help. Come, heal my old wounds and help me to see your better way! Thank you for your generous grace in redeeming my past shortcomings. Thank you for the better way that comes through honoring your standard for marriage and sex. Help me to live according to your ways.

Chapter 11

The Way of Family

"God places the lonely in families..." Psalms 68:6

About two months after my oldest son was born, we decided to make the trip to our annual family reunion in Grand Marais, MN. Our family has been gathering on the shores of Lake Superior for decades. It has become a fairy-tale-like experience for me. The rhythms of eating World's Best Donuts every morning with my parents and sister, getting Dairy Queen each evening with my cousins, and staying up late around a fire with my extended family has made the experience unrivaled in my memories of childhood. Now, I had a chance to bring my new son into this cherished tradition with us.

During this trip, my entire immediate family decided to share a cabin right outside of the quaint little downtown of Grand Marais. Since our son was only two months old, we were just learning how to be parents. Everything seemed to move slower and require more energy than it used to. Leaving the cabin had once only taken the 30 seconds required to put my shoes on. Now, it would take 10, 20, sometimes 30 minutes! After making sure our son was fed and changed, the baby bag was prepped, and getting the stroller ready, it was a profound

The Better Way

accomplishment each time we left the front door. My parents, sister, and brother-in-law, who weren't as immediately familiar with the needs of a baby, would consistently leave us in their dust each time we left the cabin.

One of these times that we were in a hurry to catch up with my family as they went out the door, I had to change my son's diaper. I put him on the edge of a padded foot rest, got the new diaper in position, and had a wet wipe ready. It was after I had taken off the old diaper and wiped him off that it happened. There was a deep rumble in his stomach followed by a loud noise. As I looked down, my son's bowels were erupting with great force. This eruption was so powerful that it squirted a steady stream of infant diarrhea out into the room.

This stream covered everything in its way, which happened to mostly be me. Horrified, I watched as my shorts were covered with my son's bowel movement. My mom, who witnessed the whole event take place, burst into laughter. Never expecting this would happen to me in my life, I was left in a daze and not sure what to do. I bumbled around trying to clean up myself, my son, and the room where everything had taken place. Needless to say, my shorts were ruined and we were significantly delayed in getting out the door.

Baby feces exploding all over actually offers a pretty accurate picture of what many people think about family. Family

The Way of Family

has been a messy experience for many of us. Relationships might have been difficult to navigate. Some of us have been deeply hurt by family. Some of us have been neglected by family. Some of us have never had a clear demonstration of a healthy family. Family dysfunction can leave us covered in debris and doing our best to clean ourselves up. The clean-up and recovery process from some families can sometimes take our entire lives. Participating in family is a risk.

Participating in family also comes at a great cost. This cost can come when our family's schedule takes priority over our own schedule. The cost can come when our own needs are put on the backburner and everyone else's needs take precedence. In the relationship structure that is family, we are often forced to take a backseat. We, as individuals, are required to give up a piece of ourselves for the sake of the family. It's this death of our own preferences and death to convenience that comes with being a part of a family.

When we only view family through that lens, it makes sense that it gets a bad rap. If all we ever see are its costs, it is no wonder the idea of family is becoming less popular. Over the past several decades, marriage, family, and children have all undergone (and are still undergoing) a radical shift in our current world. We have all anecdotally seen it, but the symptoms of this societal shift are becoming more and more obvious with time.

Across the board, people are getting married less often. The number of US Households that contained married couples declined from 75% in 1960 down to 49% in 2020.[48] The number of one-person households increased from 13% in 1960 to 28% in 2020. We are getting married less and living alone more often. More still, the number of children we are having is declining rapidly. The Total Fertility Rate, the number of children a fertile woman will have in her lifetime, decreased from 3.65 in 1960 to 1.64 in 2020.[49] Many children are often raised in homes that are not intact. As I highlighted in a previous chapter, one in three children will not grow up with their biological father in their home.[50] Family is becoming less common.

What if these more post-modern changes in our attitudes towards marriage and children have drawbacks? What if giving up on traditional family structure, while potentially obtaining more personal freedoms, comes at the expense of more important things?

Abandoning the idea of family does not come without costs. Family, marriage, and children can have profound benefits. People who are married are physically healthier, experience better mental health, are less likely to die, and even weather sickness better than those who are unmarried or divorced.[51] Children in two-parent households are more likely to receive parental attention, less likely to live in poverty in adulthood, and more likely to graduate college.[52] As mentioned in earlier chapters, boys raised without their father are more likely to end up incarcerated and without work in adulthood.[53] Flippantly forsaking marriage is costly. The throwing away of a marriage is a negative outcome for everyone.

More still, when choosing not to have children, we give up on a legacy that continues on after us. In not having children, we forfeit the ability to have a younger generation to take on the burden of caring for us in our old age. When this happens across an entire culture, we have society-wide problems that are just now being grappled with.[54] There's no one left to pay taxes, stimulate the economy, or carry on the culture of a people. Family lines end. Nations go extinct. Countries die. It's a repeat of Mouse Utopia. When we as a culture and people give up on the idea of family, we are all hurt.

This is not meant to be a soapbox but a sober recognition of the consequences that come from choosing our own way. To be frank, these consequences make sense. In the journey down our own way of living in this world, we have a tendency to reject fundamentally good things because of our short-sighted view. God, who wants humanity to flourish, instituted family for our good. Our rejection of these blessed institutions doesn't provide us with a better life, but rather it plunges us deeper into a more hollow and lonely human experience.

The Better Way

But admittedly, not everyone has had a good family experience. We might still be cleaning the poo out of our own lives that is left over from our horrific childhood. Maybe, we have never even seen a healthy family to give us a positive perspective.

So what is God's ideal for family?

As we discussed in the last chapter, God created marriage.[55] Marriage, which is meant to be filled with intimacy and trust, is the basis upon which the whole family is built. From marriage, God gives us a heavenly directive to be fruitful and multiply.[56] This multiplication, having children, is a God-given, natural by-product of marital intimacy. These children of intimacy are something God defines as an objective good.

> *"Children are a gift from the Lord; they are a reward from him. Children born to a young man are like arrows in a warrior's hands. How joyful is the man whose quiver is full of them!"* Psalm 127:3-5

God gives children as a gift to parents. They are always a blessing! Yet, how often do attitudes in our current culture talk of children as burdens or barriers? Those attitudes stand in direct opposition to God's view of children. These children, who are given to couples as gifts from God, are expected to honor their mother and father.[57] God says He will bless children who honor their parents with a long life. Just like our culture's opinion of children, how often is honoring our parents encouraged in our world? Parents are often mocked, painted as incompetent, out-of-touch fools, and criticized as impediments to our fun. Yet, God expects kids to honor their parents. And this honoring of mother and father is not meant to end at the magic age of 18 or even if we don't like our parents. Honor is always what God asks of children.

God continues to expand family by giving grandparents with grandchildren. This blessing is so strong that in Proverbs 17:6 the Bible tells us that *"Grandchildren are the crowning glory of the aged."* Just like with my grandparents on their acreage in Wisconsin, this is why grandparents love to "spoil" their grandkids and go to great lengths to show their love for them. God's unique blessing given to grandparents demonstrates that God's ideal for family is not meant to be limited to one set of parents with one set of children. Instead, God has designed family to be successive, branching generations of children, parents, grandparents, great grandparents, and so on. Families are designed to grow. Families are designed to fill homes with life from the very youngest to the most elderly.

Family is God's ideal structure for us humans to flourish. One astonishing way God uses family is to aid in the vanquishing of a long-hated enemy of humanity: loneliness. Family is one of God's best answers for loneliness:

The Better Way

"God places the lonely in families..." Psalm 68:6

Family is designed to be a gift to us. Family was created so that we did not have to live life alone. Family was given to us by God as an ideal way to experience life.

This paradigm of family is so beautiful and good because it reflects God's nature. God has designed family as a reflection of how He treats us. It is through the language of family that God describes our relationships with Him. God allows us to call Him "Father."[58] As our Father, God promises to give us, His children, good gifts[59] and to discipline us for our betterment.[60] The Bible describes the love Jesus has for us in laying down His life for us in terms of a husband loving His wife.[61] As one of my favorite speakers says, "God is a family man."[62] The earthly, human form of family is meant to provide a reflection of this Godly model. After all, we are creatures who bear God's image.[63]

Unfortunately, for many, God's ideal of family is not our story. Like I mentioned previously, family has hurt us. Family has burned us and left us wounded. Maybe we can't even be with our families for the sake of our own safety. Let me be quick to say, I'm sorry. I've seen how family can go awry first hand in people close to me. In its ability to uniquely bless us, family also has an ability to uniquely wound us. That was never God's intent for you. God's Will was not that you would be abused, betrayed, and abandoned by your family. Family, like all things in our world, has been corrupted by people going their own way. When people abandon God's way of living, their self-destructive lives often have collateral damage. Most often, that collateral damage is experienced in their family.

Though God has not intended for us to experience family that way, He is uniquely capable of redeeming what has been destroyed in our lives. God can redeem you. God can redeem an entire family. Even if your family rejects the redemption of God, God can start a new kind of family through you. Where your parents failed each other, God can use you to bless your spouse. Where your parents failed you, God can use you to bless your children. Where your family abandoned you, God can use you to be faithful to every member of your family. God can use you to establish a family that more closely resembles His ideal.

Whether getting married and having biological children is something we experience in our lives or not, no one is left out from the way of family that God prescribes. There is a call on all of our lives to honor, contribute, and participate in what family we do have. Yes, we should have healthy boundaries in the cases of extreme toxicity. But we can all still love our families as the best son, daughter, brother, sister, uncle, or aunt that we know how.

The Better Way

Furthermore, we often undervalue the family that God adopts us into in the new people He is bringing together through Jesus. God's good will for all of us is to find our place and experience His family of children called the Church. In His Church, we can find love and deep connection just like what is found in biological families, sometimes even more. Self-sacrificial love and generous affection is meant to be common in the family of God. In God's family, we can even model family well by becoming spiritual fathers and mothers to others that God puts in our care. God's best for all of us, regardless of our relationship status or household size, is found in the context of family. God's way is the way of family.

Over and over again, humanity has corrupted what was established for our good with our own selfish ways. The ways the world prescribes are never solutions. At best, they are merely band-aids that cover up the wound. At worst, like abandoning the idea of family entirely, they create new wounds for us to address. But God can heal our wounds fully. God's ways are redemptive and restorative. God's way of family is redemptive. God's way of family is what's best for us. Let us look to His ideal, His ways, because they are always better. God's plan for family is the better way.

Living the Better Way:

Consider the questions below. Let Jesus lead you into what life in His better way looks like.

1. How has my own family fallen short of God's ideal for family? How might have I been wounded in my past experience with family?

2. Is my vision for family in line with Jesus's better way? What conversations of forgiveness might I need to have? What relationships should I value differently in light of Jesus's way for family?

Turning to Jesus: Jesus, you know my family's story. Jesus, you know the unique ways my family may have failed. Come, redeem my vision of family and help me to see your better way! Thank you for your blessing on families. Thank you for the better way that comes with participating in both biological and spiritual family. Help me to live according to your ways.

Chapter 12

The Way of Faithfulness

"The master said, 'Well done, my good and faithful servant…'"
Matthew 25:23

During the depths of the great recession in late 2008 into early 2009, my dad had resigned from his position as pastor of a church he had helped start a few years earlier. Though the economy wasn't great, it was clear that the time had come for our family to move on to the next chapter of our lives. Miraculously, in the months following, my dad received not just one job offer but two job offers. First, my dad was given the opportunity to work at a financial firm in the suburbs of Minneapolis. It would be wildly different from what our family was used to, but it was a lucrative career that promised a higher pay scale than anything in the church world.

The other opportunity was to take a pastoral position at a struggling, small-town church in rural Iowa. Financially, this was the far less secure option. In terms of career prospects for my dad, it was also somewhat illogical. The church was in a small town called Estherville, hundreds of miles from where we lived, and only one quarter of the size of the church he had just resigned from. Many of my father's friends told him that taking this church position would be a huge step backwards for his career and our family. Less prestige, less money, less people. Yet, after praying it through, our entire family was somehow excited to leave the suburbs of Minneapolis and make the move to rural Iowa. It would be a decision that impacted the entire trajectory of our family.

No, my parents did not strike it rich through investing in farmland. No, my dad's career prospects did not soar. No, the church did not grow to 1,000 people. What did happen was still deeply impacting to us all. In Estherville, we experienced a wonderful community. We saw the love of Jesus change people's lives. We grew together as we experienced the common mission of representing Jesus in our little town.

For me, I was able to get my first job bagging groceries at a store in town. Eventually, I was able to complete my associate degree at the local community college during high school and obtain in-state tuition at Iowa State University. Thus, paving the way for me to get an engineering degree. At Iowa State University, I would go on to meet my wife, make some of my dearest friends, and encounter God for myself for the first time outside of my parents' home.

Hindsight shows that not only I but my sister and parents were profoundly and positively impacted by the decision to move to small-town Iowa. How is this possible? The way the world's wisdom was telling my family to go was in the complete opposite direction! So how could such an illogical decision regarding my dad's job result in such significant good for our entire family?

My conclusion is this: Faithfulness is more important in life than opportunity or influence. In living faithfully, we live in accordance with how God intended us to live.

My dad was simply faithful in the opportunity he felt like God had given us. My family did nothing more than embrace our new community and live life the best way we knew how. We made friends. We worked hard. We loved people in need. It was a humbling and slow-moving experience, but we were faithful with what we had been given. God blessing our family in our faithfulness is the sole reason why we experienced so much good during our time in Estherville.

So what is faithfulness? Faithfulness is to be full of faith, steadfast, firm in honoring promises or duty, or loyal.[64]

Faithfulness stands in contrast to much of what we have been told in measuring the significance of our lives. We have been told that our lives will only be considered successful if we get a good degree from a great college and end up in a high caliber career rather than being reliable or hardworking. We have been trained to think that the dollars in our bank accounts are a better measure of our worth than our integrity behind closed doors. We have been inculcated with the idea that our influence is better measured in followers/subscribers/views rather than with the health of our family. In its own corrupted way, the world has redefined success as lofty achievement in the superficial rather than faithfulness in the fundamental.

A story that Jesus told in Matthew 25 illustrates God's way of faithfulness perfectly. A master had three servants to which he entrusted some of his fortune with before he left on a long trip. The master gave one servant five talents, to another two talents, and to another servant one talent. A talent is an amount of money worth about 20 years of labor.[65] An enormous amount of money! The master's assumption was that his servants would steward his money well in his absence.

Upon the master's return, he summoned his servants. The servants with five talents and with two talents had doubled the money their master had entrusted to them. The master replied in Matthew 25:23, *"Well done, my good and faithful servant. You have been faithful in handling this small amount, so now I will give you many more responsibilities. Let's celebrate together!"* The master was pleased with how these servants had faithfully used their talents.

The servant with one talent came with a different story. This servant had merely returned the talent to his master after having buried it in the ground for the entirety of his master's absence. He had literally hidden his talent in a hole and covered it up with dirt. The master called this servant "wicked and lazy."[66] The master was severe but just in his assessment of the servant. The master, then, had the servant thrown out of the household. Ouch.

There are two important lessons that we should take away from this story regarding faithfulness. First, we are going to be judged with how we have wisely or unwisely handled the things in our life God has given to us. We will be evaluated with how faithful we were with what we have been given. That might feel unfair if we compare ourselves with people who are more gifted. We might think, "People have been given so much more than me!" or "I wasn't given a good childhood" or "I don't have much money or resources." Our self-evaluations may be very true, but that's why the second takeaway is critical.

Second, notice the master's reaction to both the servants with two talents and five talents. His reaction was the same! The initial number of talents given to the servants nor the absolute number of talents profited by the servant in the end changed the pleasure of the master. For both the five-talent servant and the two-talent servant, the master responded by calling them "good and faithful."[67] Their faithfulness to what was given to them is what pleased the master, not the initial number of talents they were given. Conversely, it wasn't the fact that the one-talent servant had only been given one talent that aroused the anger of the master. The master's anger was at the servant's unfaithfulness to that single talent. Again, he had buried it in the ground!

What does that mean for us? In the midst of a world that draws us deep into the game of comparison to others, our success and value in this world is not dependent upon what we may or may not have. Our success is only determined by whether we have been faithful with what we have been given. This is a beautiful reality. If you were born rich, that does not determine God's approval of your life. If you were born poor, that does not determine God's approval of your life. Whether you consider yourself intelligent or unintelligent, that does not determine God's approval of your life. God's definition of success for our lives is faithfulness to what we have been given.

It is in what is most fundamental in our lives where faithfulness is most clearly demonstrated. Faithfulness looks like a husband saying "no" to all other women and only saying "yes" to his wife. Faithfulness looks like being a reliable friend to someone when they're in crisis. Faithfulness looks like being a good student in school. Faithfulness looks like working hard at our jobs. Faithfulness looks like choosing to honor God even when we might be embarrassed. Faithfulness is simple and uncomplicated. Most of the time it's pretty boring. Faithfulness is revealed in the fundamental and basic aspects of our lives.

The Way of Faithfulness

But here's the hard part. It takes a lifetime to prove ourselves as faithful people. At the same time, unfaithfulness is demonstrated in a single moment. While faithfulness is confirmed throughout the entirety of our lives, it can all be blown in an instant. A man only has to cheat on his wife once to be considered unfaithful. We only have to fail to defend our friend one time to be considered a bad friend. It only takes one day to get fired from a job and be considered an irresponsible worker. It's because of this years-long aspect of faithfulness that it is so difficult to be people who are faithful.

When thinking about success in our life, the question of our own personal significance inevitably comes up. We all want to live a life of significance. But what does that word even mean? If we let God define it, then faithfulness becomes the answer. Significance doesn't mean speaking to stadiums or a YouTube account with 1 million subscribers. Nor does it necessarily mean starting the largest non-profit in the world that feeds hungry people. A life of significance is one found faithful. As one of my dear friends pointedly challenges me with: "If your life only consists of loving God and loving your family, and nothing more, is that enough for you?"[68] A life of faithfulness would reply, "Absolutely, yes."

Faithfulness is our measuring rod of success and significance.

The Better Way

Amazingly, the Bible teaches that it is through a life of faithfulness that we will see the greatest amount of fruitfulness. It is only through steadfastness and unwavering commitment throughout our lives that we will see real success. This is especially true when choosing to live our lives following Jesus. Jesus says in John 15:5, *"Those who remain in me and I in them, will produce much fruit."* Fruitfulness follows faithfulness. And Jesus is only confirming this principle that has already been set out in other parts of the Bible:

"A faithful person will be richly blessed, but one eager to get rich will not go unpunished." Proverbs 28:20

"If you are faithful in little things, you will be faithful in large ones. But if you are dishonest in little things, you won't be honest with greater responsibilities." Luke 16:10

Notice how faithfulness does not equal perfection. Faithfulness is being diligent in our responsibilities. Faithfulness is doing the best we can, when we can, with what we have been given. This doesn't necessarily mean we have to perfectly perform throughout our lives. It means we only have to be faithful, and God will take care of the rest. He, alone, measures our faithfulness because He knows our hearts. God doesn't care about the results if He knows we have been faithful to what He gave us. That means if we are faithful, we can trust him with the outcomes, or the fruit, of our lives. What wonderful news!

The Way of Faithfulness

The way of the world stands in stark contrast to the way of faithfulness. The world tells us that it's okay if successful people cut corners, betray others, or are unfaithful in their commitments. The world anxiously tells us that we have to rack up the achievements to be significant. The world fills us with fear that if we aren't successful now, then we won't ever be successful. The world pressures us to perform so perfectly that we should run people over who might be standing in the way of our perfect performance. That worldly measure of success of significance will result in unfaithfulness. That worldly understanding of success can only bring pain into our lives. That measure of value will cause us to short circuit the profound good that comes from a life lived in faithfulness.

Instead, the measure of faithfulness tells us success comes from being consistent in the little things in front of us now. The way of faithfulness orients our lives around a measure proven over a lifetime, not in our current position. The way of faithfulness gives us rest in knowing that our role is to live in a way that honors what we have been given and that God will bring the increase. The way of faithfulness gives us the healthier measure of doing what we can as best as we can, not flawless perfection. Instead of our lives being measured in a singular moment, our success is now measured in a lifetime of faithfulness. Faithfulness is the better measure of one's life. Faithfulness is the better way of living.

Living the Better Way:

Consider the questions below. Let Jesus lead you into what life in His better way looks like.

1. Have I been faithful with the small things God has given me in my life? In what areas of my life might I be found unfaithful?

2. How might I define my life's significance differently? What does trying to live a life of faithfulness look like for my life now?

Turning to Jesus: Jesus, thank you for still loving unfaithful people, like I sometimes am. Jesus, you know the ways I have been unfaithful in my life. Come, show me how to be faithful and help me live in your better way! Thank you for the opportunities and blessings that exist in my life. Thank you for the better way that comes through being faithful in everything you have given me. Help me to live according to your ways.

Chapter 13

The Way Is the Destination

"Now this is eternal life: that they know you, the only true God, and Jesus Christ, whom you have sent." John 17:3 (NIV)

One of my favorite things to do is to travel and plan trips. Putting all the details together, getting the best deals on flights or places to stay, and finding the exotic locations to travel to is a thrilling experience for me. So when my wife and I got married, I asked Katie if I could plan our honeymoon. Taking an even bigger risk, I asked her if I could plan the honeymoon and surprise her with it. Knowing my excitement about trips, she said, "Yes."

With great excitement, I started to do my research on what would be the perfect place to travel to based on our preferences as a couple. I looked incessantly at flights to find the best deal. Then one Tuesday morning in the final months prior to our wedding, I found the perfect flights. For a ridiculously cheap price during July, I found ideal flights from Chicago O'Hare to Geneva, Switzerland. Before I purchased the tickets, I called Katie and told her that I was going to make the move to buy the tickets (even though she didn't know where to yet). After getting off the phone, I bought the tickets. Then, I moved on to

The Better Way

planning out our two-week-long trip to Switzerland, northern Italy, and eastern France. About two months prior to our wedding, I had the car booked, flights purchased, and three different Airbnb's across those countries reserved. All that was left to do was keep the secret for another 60 days.

As our wedding got closer, I told a few select people about where we were going so they could make sure we were safe. Besides that, no one knew, and Katie still did not know. Two days after our wedding, we got on our flight from Chicago O'Hare to our connection in Washington DC. All Katie knew, even on that first flight, was that we had a layover in DC and that she needed her passport. While we were in the air, our flight experienced significant delays. Instead of having a relaxed 2-hour layover, I wasn't even sure if we were going to make our flight to Geneva. Only if we sprinted through the airport could we make it to our next plane in time. As we landed in DC, I told Katie the gate of our next flight and finally revealed the destination that we were headed to. We madly dashed through the DC airport and incredibly made our flight!

On the next flight to Switzerland, I enthusiastically told Katie all the details of our trip. I showed her pictures of our Airbnb's, the locations on a map of Europe that we were going to, and the exciting things we were going to get to do. After our plane arrived in Geneva, we got our quirky little European rental car. Then, we drove three hours across the Swiss Alps into

The Way Is the Destination

northern Italy. Along the shores of Lake Maggiore, we got to spend the first six nights of our honeymoon. To say it was a memorable experience is an understatement. We were able to see a massive lake with towering mountains as its backdrop out all of our windows. We could see palm trees and glacier-capped peaks in the same view. We had fantastic food and adventured through some of the most breathtaking landscapes we had ever seen. We had a wonderful honeymoon.

Now, our trip was amazing. In my opinion, I had honed my trip planning skills to craft the perfect vacation. Our location gave us great views, great weather, and great food. Yet, here is the wonderful truth of our honeymoon. The real destination wasn't northern Italy. The real destination of our honeymoon wasn't even the rest of eastern France and Switzerland that we would go on to explore. The actual destination of our honeymoon was this new life together as husband and wife. The real purpose of our trip was to embark into this new reality together. Our reason for our travel was to know each other in a more true and intimate way. The potential of a life with one another that had taken hold of our hearts was now getting to be lived out.

The same is true in this new way we experience in Jesus. Yes, Jesus gives us a blueprint for a better way of living here on Earth. Yes, God's ways for us to live are inherently better than the ways of the world. Yes, God's wisdom in living is born out in a healthier, more fruitful life here on Earth. But that is not the ultimate purpose of God coming to Earth in the form of a man. Jesus came to be the way to a better life for us because He, Himself, is the life.[69] Though Jesus is the way to life, knowing Him is the definition of life itself.

"Now this is eternal life: that they know you, the only true God, and Jesus Christ, whom you have sent." John 17:3 (NIV)

This is what the entirety of our human experience is meant for. We were created for this reason - to know God. It's the very purpose of our lives. Though Jesus is certainly the way to true life, the Bible literally calls Him, "eternal life."[70]

Jesus isn't just our Way; He is our destination. Knowing Him is our greatest way of living.

The Way is our destination.

To many of us, this sounds like a cop out. How can a person be a destination? How can a single relationship be what we are created for? Those questions would be justified if that relationship was with a human. Those questions would be valid if that person was only some sort of angelic being. But that is not who God is.

The Way Is the Destination

He is God. He is Creator.[71] He is the beginning and the end.[72] Through Him and for Him, all things were created.[73] He holds all of creation together.[74] He is supreme.[75] He is first in all things.[76] The Earth and everything in it are His.[77] He knows all things.[78] He sees all things.[79] Nothing is too hard for Him.[80] His words never fail.[81] He always accomplishes His purposes.[82]

God, who is as powerful in every way, is also uniquely good. He is slow to anger.[83] He is patient.[84] He is abounding in love.[85] He is gracious.[86] He is compassionate.[87] He remembers us.[88] He is mindful of us.[89] And He wants no one to be destroyed.[90] It is because of His unique goodness that God chooses to do what no one else could ever do. God chose to rescue us after we went our own way.

Jesus, who is the exact imprint of God[91] in human form, chose to step into the greatest position of humility by dying on the cross.[92] This righteous judge, who can justly send souls to hell, does the unthinkable. He pulled us back from the brink of destruction through His own death. Jesus chose reconciliation with us at the expense of the His own life.[93] It is through this wild act of kindness towards us that we can know what real love is.[94] He has proved that His intentions towards us are exceedingly good.

Consider those realities written above for a second. The person who breathed the universe into existence is the same person who chose to die for you. The same person who created all things for Himself, left heaven behind for us. What kind of person is that?

That person is the One with whom we are invited into relationship! Jesus is the One who lavishes His great love on us.[95] He is the one that chooses to come live with us in the everyday of life. He is the One we can call friend[96], counselor[97], and Father.[98] He is the One in whom we are invited to experience eternal life through knowing Him personally.

Yet, here is the difficult-to-reconcile reality about many who say they follow Jesus: We have a tendency to reduce Jesus to a means to our own end. We often cheapen Him into being just a way to accomplish our plans. We degrade His love as a ticket into heaven or into a life that we want. If we are honest, we probably have all done this in some way that is evidenced in how we pray, the plans we make, or the way we treat God's generosity in our lives. This ought not be.

Think of it this way: How tragic would it have been if I treated my new wife this way on our honeymoon? What if I had looked at Katie on the first day of our honeymoon and said, "Great! Thanks for getting me here. I'm really glad you were with me until this point, but your services are no longer needed." Not only would that be a horrific act of selfishness, but it would reveal how awful of a husband I am. I would have manipulated

The Way Is the Destination

my new wife just as a means of experiencing a fun trip rather than someone I get the privilege of living the rest of my life with. Yet, that is what so many of us do with Jesus.

This new way of following Jesus is far better than manipulating an all powerful being into doing what we want Him to do. This way is actually an entirely new life with Him, the very One who was gracious enough to love us even when we were far off from Him. One of the writers of the New Testament, the Apostle Paul, speaks of his new life with Christ this way:

> "*I once thought these things were valuable, but now I consider them worthless because of what Christ has done. Yes, everything else is worthless when compared with the infinite value of knowing Christ Jesus my Lord. For his sake I have discarded everything else, counting it all as garbage, so that I could gain Christ and become one with him...*" Philippians 3:7-9

Paul is absolutely correct here. Everything else is worthless in comparison to knowing and being with Jesus. Everything could be discarded from our lives and being one with Him would still be better. He is that good. He is that loving. He is that wonderful.

We can absolutely live a better life by experiencing freedom and fullness in His ways. We can certainly experience deeper relationships and richer community in Jesus's prescribed ways of living for us. His ways will undoubtedly lead us into a life of intimacy and healthier family. Jesus unquestionably intends for us to experience the blessing of faithfulness. Yet, all of those ways of living fall short of knowing the person who gave us those very ways. A good life, a loving family, a healthy marriage, a stable state of mind, and living in freedom are not our destination. Jesus is.

Jesus is not the means to our specific dream. He is not the means to the specific outcome we are seeking. He is not merely the means to our happiness. He is not even the means to our deepest level of satisfaction.

No, Jesus is the very end in and of itself.

There is no greater place for us to arrive at. There is no greater destination for us to get to. There is no greater end.

Knowing Jesus is our destination.

Living the Better Way:

Consider the questions below. Let Jesus lead you into what life in His better way looks like.

1. Have I viewed knowing God as my greatest goal in this life? What might be something that I have valued more than knowing God?

2. How might my life look differently if knowing God is my highest goal? How might I approach God differently knowing that He is far more than just a means to my own end?

Turning to Jesus: Jesus, you are good. Jesus, you are loving and perfect in every way. Come, show me how to love you more and help me to see you as the better way! Thank you for giving me the opportunity to even know you. Thank you for the better way that comes with living life in relationship with you. Help me to live with you and according to your ways.

Conclusion

"...in all your ways submit to him and he will make your paths straight."
Proverbs 3:6 (NIV)

As I have had the privilege of spending so much time on the campus of Iowa State University and with university-aged individuals, I've been shocked at the tragic stories that play out in front of me. There are many individuals who, in their most vulnerable states, were sexually assaulted. Now, they are left trying to pick up the pieces. I've been appalled at the number of people burdened by the weight of anxiety and depression. I've even talked to students who have gone entire weeks without talking to another soul. Too many of my friends have ended up in the hospital from self-harm and suicidal ideation because they see no hope. My heart has been wrenched as I've seen so many self-destructively pursue pleasure after pleasure because they've been deceived into believing it's their ticket to happiness. They are longing to just fill the void of their empty lives. The tragedy of Mouse Utopia becoming the human experience has manifested before my eyes.

In response to all of this, a prayer has arisen from my heart for my city, my campus, and my friends. "LORD, show them that there is a better way!" Jesus is the only one who can truly fill people's empty lives. Their dead ways of living can be

The Better Way

exchanged for His better way of living. We all need to be awakened to the reality that humanity does not have to remain stuck in its dead ways. The way of Jesus leads us to life!

But so many do not know of Jesus's way that will lead to life. They remain trapped, often alone, and without any hope. They do not know of the way that leads to life. How can this be? How can our friends, our classmates, our professors, our bosses, and our families not know of this better way? How can they not know of this way that leads to life?

It's simple: We simply haven't told them.

I haven't told them yet. You haven't told them yet. They just haven't heard yet.

Jesus has paid a high price for all to experience life. The curse of sin and death that holds power over each life has been broken. The tight grip of shame and condemnation has been loosened. Jesus has provided a way out for our friends and family. His way to life has been opened to our peers, bosses, and neighbors. Now, there is only one thing left to be done in order for them to potentially experience this new life: We need to tell them about it. That part of this new way of life isn't on Jesus, it is on us.

Conclusion

"And then he told them, 'Go into all the world and preach the Good News to everyone." Mark 16:15

Maybe, we have just been too distracted with our favorite shows and video games to tell them. Maybe, we have been too busy with our full schedules to explain. Maybe, our lives have been too polluted by the ways of this world for them to even notice that there's an alternative. Worse still, maybe we love our dignity and ability to look good more than we love our friends.

Regardless of the reason, the way to life remains open. Today, we still have a chance to tell them about the better way found in Jesus. But our tomorrow is not guaranteed. Our friends might not be here next week. Our family members could be gone next month. The day of Jesus's return is approaching. We must make the most of every opportunity.[99] The way to life will not stay open forever. But as of today, it still is.

My charge to us all is this: *May we choose to live life Jesus's way. May our lives reflect the good that can only come from this better way. May we never lose sight of the death we were saved from when we chose Jesus's way. And may we be found pleading with our friends in great love saying, "There is a better way!*

Notes

Chapter 1
[1] (Calhoun 1973)
[2] (Calhoun 1973)
[3] (Calhoun 1973)
[4] (U.S. Census Bureau 2010)
[5] (Wilcox, Wang and ElHage 2022)
[6] (Willingham 2023)
[7] (Rothwell, Scarred Boys, Idle Men: Family Adversity, Poor Health, and Male Labor Force Participation 2023)
[8] (Barker, et al. 2023)
[9] (Barker, et al. 2023)
[10] (Wilcox, Wang and ElHage 2022)
[11] (FRED Economic Data 2023)

Chapter 4
[12] Exodus 31:18

Chapter 6
[13] Matthew 13:44 is referenced here.
[14] (Guzik 2018)

Chapter 7
[15] At a 2023 Chi Alpha Retreat, I heard Matt Carpenter of UCA Chi Alpha present this idea.
[16] (Nielsen 2023)
[17] (Rothwell, Teens Spend Average of 4.8 Hours on Social Media Per Day 2023)
[18] (Robb-Dover 2023)
[19] (National Institute On Alcohol Abuse and Alcoholism 2023)
[20] (National Institute of Health 2022)
[21] Luke 19:1-10: The Story of Zacchaeus
[22] Luke 7:37 and John 8:1-11
[23] John 21:25

Chapter 8
[24] (Paul 2019)
[25] (Twenge, et al. 2010)
[26] (Ivey-Stephenson, et al. 2022)
[27] (Ivey-Stephenson, et al. 2022)

Chapter 9
[28] Psalm 23:5
[29] (Cox 2021)
[30] (Heinze, et al. 2023)
[31] (Center For Disease Control and Prevention 2023)
[32] (US Surgeon General 2023)
[33] Matthew 6:15
[34] Galatians 6:2
[35] Colossians 3:13
[36] Philippians 2:3
[37] Romans 12:10
[38] Hebrews 10:24-5

Chapter 10
[39] (Strong 1990)
[40] Matthew 19:10
[41] Matthew 19:12
[42] (World Population Review 2024)
[43] (Wang 2023)
[44] (Knopp, et al. 2017, Knopp, et al. 2017)
[45] https://www.ncbi.nlm.nih.gov/pmc/articles/PMC8465630/
[46] (Cranney 2020)
[47] (Willoughby, et al. 2023)

Chapter 11
[48] (VanOrman and Jacobsen 2020)
[49] (FRED Economic Data 2023)
[50] (U.S. Census Bureau 2010)
[51] (Hughes and Waite 2009)

Notes

[52] (W. B. Wilcox, et al. 2023)
[53] (Wilcox, Wang and ElHage 2022)
[54] Japan is the society most notably experiencing this kind of decline.
[55] Genesis 2:24
[56] Genesis 1:28
[57] Exodus 20:12
[58] Matthew 6:9
[59] Matthew 7:11
[60] Hebrews 12:6-8
[61] Ephesians 5:25
[62] Michael Dow – This is a saying not to cheapen God's heavenly capabilities but to bring His nature into more familiar language.
[63] Genesis 1:26

Chapter 12
[64] (Merriam-Webster 2024)
[65] Matthew 25:15 English Standard Version footnotes.
[66] Matthew 25:26
[67] Matthew 25:21,23
[68] Pastor Drew Meyer of LifePointe Church in Ames, Iowa

Chapter 13
[69] John 11:25
[70] 1 John 1:2
[71] Genesis 1:1
[72] Revelation 1:8
[73] Colossians 1:16
[74] Colossians 1:17
[75] Colossians 1:18
[76] Colossians 1:18
[77] Psalm 24:1
[78] 1 John 3:20
[79] Hebrews 4:13
[80] Genesis 18:14
[81] Luke 1:37
[82] Isaiah 55:11

[83] Exodus 34:6
[84] 2 Peter 3:9
[85] Exodus 34:6
[86] Psalm 103:8
[87] Psalm 103:8
[88] Psalm 136:23
[89] Psalm 8:4
[90] 2 Peter 3:9
[91] Hebrews 1:3
[92] Philippians 2:8
[93] Colossians 1:20
[94] 1 John 3:16
[95] 1 John 1:3
[96] John 15:15
[97] John 15:26
[98] Matthew 6:19

Conclusion
[99] Ephesians 5:15-16

References

American College Health Association. 2023. *National College Health Assessment*. American College Health Association.

Barker, Gary, Caroline Hayes, Brian Heilman, and Michael Reichert. 2023. "State of American Men 2023." *Equimundo*. Accessed January 29, 2024. https://www.equimundo.org/wp-content/uploads/2023/05/STATE-OF-AMERICAN-MEN-2023.pdf.

Calhoun, John B. 1973. "Death Squared: The Explosive Growth and Demise of a Mouse Population." *Proceedings of the Royal Society of Medicine* 80-89.

Center For Disease Control and Prevention. 2023. "Health Risks of Social Isolation and Loneliness." *Center For Disease Control and Prevention*. March 30. Accessed January 9, 2024. https://www.cdc.gov/emotional-wellbeing/social-connectedness/loneliness.htm.

Cox, Daniel A. 2021. "The State of American Friendship: Change, Challenges, and Loss." *American Survey Center*. June 8. Accessed January 2023, 9. https://www.americansurveycenter.org/research/the-state-of-american-friendship-change-challenges-and-loss/.

Cranney, Stephen. 2020. "The Influence of Religiosity/Spirituality on Sex Life Satisfaction and Sexual Frequency: Insights from the Baylor Religion Survey." *Review of Religious Research* 289-314.

FRED Economic Data - St Louis Fed. 2023. *Fertility Rate, Total for the United States.* May 9. Accessed January 19, 2024.

https://fred.stlouisfed.org/series/SPDYNTFRTINUSA.

FRED Economic Data. 2023. *Fertility Rate, Total for the United States.* May 9.

https://fred.stlouisfed.org/series/SPDYNTFRTINUSA.

Guzik, David. 2018. *Colossians 3 - Put Off, Put On.*

https://enduringword.com/bible-commentary/colossians-3/.

Heinze, Justin, Sarah Ketchen Lipson, Daniel Eisenberg, and Sarah Zhou. 2023. "The Healthy Minds Study: 2022-2023 Data Report." The Healthy Minds Network.

Hughes, Mary Elizabeth, and Linda J Waite. 2009. "Marital Biography and Health at Mid-Life." *Journal of Health and Social Behavior* 344-358.

Ivey-Stephenson, Asha Z, Alex E Crosby, Jennifer M Hoenig, Shiromani Gyawali, Eunice Park-Lee, and Sara L Hedden. 2022. *Suicidal Thoughts and Behaviors Among Adults Aged ≥18 Years — United States, 2015–2019.* January 7. Accessed January 8, 2024.

https://www.cdc.gov/mmwr/volumes/71/ss/ss7101a1.htm.

Knopp, Kayla, Shelby Scott, Lane Ritchie, Galena K Rhoades, Howard J Markman, and Scott M Stanely. 2017. "Once a Cheater, Always a Cheater? Serial Infidelity Across Subsequent Relationships." *Archives of Sexual Behavior* 2301-2311. Accessed January 27, 2024.

https://psychcentral.com/blog/how-common-is-cheating-infidelity-really.

MacLellan, Lila. 2019. "Maslow's pyramid of needs." *Quartz*, April 19.

Merriam-Webster. 2024. *faithful*. Accessed January 24, 2024.

https://www.merriam-webster.com/dictionary/faithfulness.

Notes

National Institute of Health. 2022. "Marijuana and hallucinogen use among young adults reached all-time high in 2021." *National Institute of Health.* August 22. https://www.nih.gov/news-events/news-releases/marijuana-hallucinogen-use-among-young-adults-reached-all-time-high-2021.

National Institute On Alcohol Abuse and Alcoholism. 2023. "Alcohol Use in the United States: Age Groups and Demographic Characteristics." *National Institute On Alcohol Abuse and Alcoholism.* https://www.niaaa.nih.gov/alcohols-effects-health/alcohol-topics/alcohol-facts-and-statistics/alcohol-use-united-states-age-groups-and-demographic-characteristics.

Nielsen. 2023. "Connectivity is driving how Americans are engaging with TV." *Nielsen.* March. https://www.nielsen.com/insights/2023/connectivity-is-driving-how-americans-are-engaging-with-tv/.

Paul, Susan. 2019. "Understanding Why You Hit "The Wall"." *Runner's World.* April 12. https://www.runnersworld.com/training/a20854502/understanding-why-you-hit-the-wall/.

Robb-Dover, Kristina. 2023. "Revealing Statistics Re: Pornography Addiction." *FHE Health.* January 15. https://fherehab.com/learning/pornography-addiction-stats.

Rothwell, Jonathan. 2023. "Scarred Boys, Idle Men: Family Adversity, Poor Health, and Male Labor Force Participation." *Institute For Family Studies.* January 17. Accessed January 29, 2024. https://ifstudies.org/blog/scarred-boys-idle-men-family-adversity-poor-health-and-male-labor-force-participation#:~:text=Men%2C%20Research%20Brief-,Young%20and%20middle%2Daged%20American%20men%20are%20less%20likely%20to,Labor%20Statistics%27%20Current%20P.

Rothwell, Jonathan. 2023. "Teens Spend Average of 4.8 Hours on Social Media Per Day." *Gallup.* October 13. https://news.gallup.com/poll/512576/teens-spend-average-hours-social-media-per-day.aspx.

Strong, James. 1990. *The New Strong's Exhaustive Concordance of the Bible.* Nashville: Thomas Nelson Publishers.

Twenge, Jean M, Brittany Gentile, C. Nathan DeWall, Debbie Ma, Katharine Lacefield, and David R Schurtz. 2010. "Birth cohort increases in psychopathology among young Americans, 1938-2007: A cross-temporal meta-analysis of the MMPI." *Clinical Psychology Review* 145-154.

U.S. Census Bureau. 2010. *Current Survey ""Living Arrangements of Children under 18 Years/1 and Marital Status of Parents by Age, Sex, Race, and Hispanic Origin/2 and Selected Characteristics of the Child for all Children 2010".* US Census Bureau.

U.S. Surgeon General. 2023. *Our Epidemic of Loneliness and Isolation.* US Public Health Service.

VanOrman, Alicia, and Linda A Jacobsen. 2020. "U.S. Household Composition Shifts as the Population Grows Older; More Young Adults Live With Parents." *Population Referencec Bureau.* February 12. Accessed January 19, 2024. https://www.prb.org/resources/u-s-household-composition-shifts-as-the-population-grows-older-more-young-adults-live-with-parents/.

Notes

Wang, Wendy. 2023. "The U.S. Marriage Rate Rebounds to Its Pre-Pandemic Level." *Institute for Family Studies.* September 15. Accessed January 27, 2024. https://ifstudies.org/blog/the-us-marriage-rate-rebounds-to-its-pre-pandemic-level.

Wilcox, W Bradford, Wendy Wang, Spencer James, and Thomas Murray. 2023. "Do Two Parents Matter More Than Ever?" *Institute For Family Studies.* September 20. Accessed January 19, 2024. https://ifstudies.org/blog/do-two-parents-matter-more-than-ever.

Wilcox, W. Bradford, Wendy Wang, and Alysse ElHage. 2022. "'Life Without Father': Less College, Less Work, and More Prison for Young Men Growing Up Without Their Biological Father." *Institute for Family Studies.* June 17. https://ifstudies.org/blog/life-without-father-less-college-less-work-and-more-prison-for-young-men-growing-up-without-their-biological-father.

Willingham, AJ. 2023. *What does the term 'Incel' mean?* March 16. https://www.cnn.com/2023/03/16/us/incel-involuntary-celibate-explained-cec/index.html.

Willoughby, Brian J, Jason S Carrol, Carson Dover, and Jessica T Sullivan. 2023. *The Myth of Sexual Experience.* Wheatley Institute.

World Population Review. 2024. *Average Number of Sexual Partners by Country 2024.* Accessed January 27, 2024. https://worldpopulationreview.com/country-rankings/average-number-of-sexual-partners-by-country.

Acknowledgements

In the writing and publishing of this book, I have been humbled by the many members of my community who dedicated their time, effort, and energy to seeing this through. I want to make sure I recognize and thank those who have contributed. Firstly, my wife, Katie, who has helped me experience so many of these better realities of Jesus in my own life. Thank you for your self-sacrificial love for our family and willingness to obey God in whatever He calls us to. I also want to thank my father, Travis Rosinger, and my dear friend, Pastor Drew Meyer, who both have contributed so much not only to my life in the Lord, but also to this project. Natalie Pratt, a friend and Chi Alpha alumnus, who proof-read and edited this book in the midst of her own ministry priorities. Lastly, I want to thank my sister, Samantha Gades, for the creative energy she contributed by designing the stunning covers for this book.

About the Author

Alex Rosinger is the director of a campus ministry, partnered with LifePointe Church, reaching the campus of Iowa State University. In the heat of 2020, Alex and his wife Katie moved states, leaving their fields of work to instead love and disciple college students on the campus of their alma mater. Their hearts are committed to seeing Jesus transform the thousands of lives of university students on their campus. Alex and Katie love the life God has given them to live in Ames, Iowa with their three young boys Winston, Theodore, and Peter.

Made in the USA
Monee, IL
29 September 2024

66443816R00095